Using The American Quarter Horse

"Using Th

American Quarter Horse

by

L. N. Sikes

with Bob Gray

Published by

The Saddlerock Corporation

This book was designed by Owen Trebeck.

Library of Congress catalogue card No. 58-59930
Second Edition

Printed in the United States of America

This book is dedicated to all my friends who love horses—and anyone who loves horses is my friend.

—L. N. SIKES

TABLE OF CONTENTS

INTRODUCTION

No breed of horse in America's history has come so far, so fast, nor been used for so many things, as the American Quarter Horse.

The breed that had no official name, registry or status 20 years ago has, in less than one decade:

1) Become the nation's most popular horse for work and sport,

2) Created a horse-breeding and selling industry of national proportions,

3) Started a new kind of riding and "performance" competition now popular in 33 states, and

4) Turned thousands of non-riding urbanites into part-time cowboys—and pretty good ones, at that.

In every state and in 20 foreign countries you will find Quarter Horses on farms and ranches, working. You will find them at rodeos, horse shows, contests and race tracks, competing.

The breed nationally has doubled in size in five years. It is growing twice as fast as any major horse breed in North America. More important, the Quarter Horse has made riding and horse show contestants out of people who never cared about horses before.

Go to any Quarter Horse show, anywhere in the United States—and they're not hard to find. (Some 354 Quarter Horse shows were held in 33 states in 1957) You will see doctors and lawyers, druggists and grocers, merchants, mechanics and engineers riding well-trained Quarter Horses in some form of western-style competition. You'll see teen-aged boys and girls

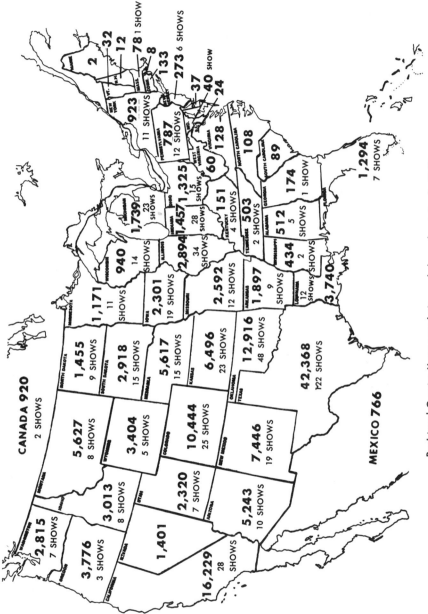

Registered Quarter Horse population and shows, by states, in 1959

in barrel races. You may see their mothers and grandmothers in there too.

These new riders, owners and contestants have made themselves known in many ways: They're buying good Quarter Horses at public sales and direct from breeders—and buying them so fast that the average reported sale price almost doubled from 1956 to 1957.*

They're subscribing to western horse magazines in growing numbers and at least one-third of such readers live in towns and cities.

They're buying saddles, bridles, hats, boots, horse trailers, horseshoes, and blankets so fast that new manufacturers have jumped into the field while old ones continue to enjoy a rising level of business.

Everywhere, including northern and eastern states, the growth of western riding and the Quarter Horse breed has caused formation of Quarter Horse associations and has spurred the organizing of annual shows, contests, and exhibitions.

How do you explain this growth of western riding interest? For one thing, people undoubtedly have more leisure time and income than ever before. The growth of relatively expensive pastimes like boating and sports car use bears this out.

There is television and the growing popularity of rodeo to remind many people of the pleasure, sport, and good exercise available outdoors on horseback.

There is also, in many areas, a steady movement on the part of upper-middle class families to outlying, semi-rural suburbs—where the keeping and use of horses is comparatively simple. In such areas, high school, FFA and Youth rodeos have put children on Quarter Horses who would not otherwise become interested in riding.

These factors, then, help explain the following tables. Table I shows a growth comparison, in terms of annual registrations

---

* From a 26 sale average of $597 in 1956 to a 28 sale average of $1,005 in 1957.

for the nation's major purebred horse breeds as reported to The Breeder's Gazette:

Year	Quarter Horse	Thorough- bred	Shetland	Standard- bred	Saddle- bred	Tenn. Walk. Horse	Arab.
1957	21,552	10,407	5,743	4,775	2,100	1,600	1,114
1956	16,951	9,774	5,163	4,600	1,541	1,650	918
1955	12,725	9,186	3,758	4,512	2,055	1,350	840
1954	11,123	8,483	2,553	4,496	2,368	1,239	763
1953	12,868	8,720	2,827	4,885	2,216	1,250	805

TABLE II

This table of ownership transfers shows the increase in Quarter Horse buying and selling:*

1957..........17,449		1954.......... 6,681
1956..........12,787		1953.......... 6,072
1955.......... 8,881		1952.......... 5,127

Yet, in spite of the breed's astonishing growth, most Americans probably still do not have clear understanding of exactly what a Quarter Horse is, does or looks like.

Ask some non-riding friend to explain what a Quarter Horse is and you'll get an answer something like this:

"Isn't it a horse than can run real fast for a quarter of a mile?"

The name of the Quarter Horse breed does suggest the racehorse. Yet, of more than 150,000 American Quarter Horses now registered in 21 nations, only 1,663 competed on recognized Quarter running tracks in 1957—just over one per cent of the total.

This book, therefore, is designed not only as a practical guide to help horsemen get more performance, pleasure and profit from their Quarter Horses, but also to explain the Quarter Horse—where it came from, what the breed looks like, what it can be used for, and how.

The reader may notice that the bulk of this book is written like horsemen talk. This is no accident.

---

*Compiled by the American Quarter Horse Association.

Largely, the text is in L. N. Sikes' own words. They were tape recorded, transcribed to paper, then organized into chapters.

Most of his figures of speech have been carefully retained. As an example, horses generally are called "him" or "he"—unless the horse in question is a mare. This is because Sikes, like most horsemen, thinks of the horse in masculine terms.

This approach was adopted because we are primarily interested in being understood. The spoken language of Western America is a clear, easily handled medium of communication. We could see no good reason why it shouldn't be put on paper just about the way it is talked.

You may be entertained by much of what you read here. However, the humor in this book is included simply because it is a basic part of the lasting fun a horseman usually gets from his experiences. Our primary purpose is still to inform and instruct.

As the Quarter Horse is a "using horse," so is this designed to be a "using book."

Saddlerock Corporation
Dayton, Texas
December 1, 1960

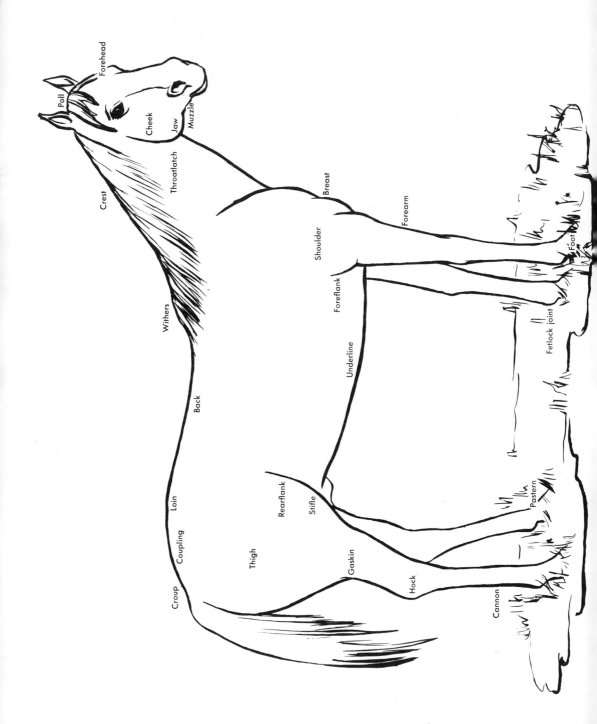

Forehead
Poll
Cheek
Jaw
Muzzle
Crest
Throatlatch
Breast
Shoulder
Forearm
Foot
Foreflank
Withers
Fetlock joint
Underline
Back
Pastern
Loin
Rearflank
Stifle
Coupling
Thigh
Gaskin
Croup
Hock
Cannon

1   BREED CHARACTERISTICS

Quarter Horses are not big horses. They'll stand a little over 14 hands high, where most Thoroughbreds will stand 15-16 hands high. Quarter Horses are stout and well-muscled. They'll weigh between 900 and 1,200 pounds.

Two other main ways to recognize the Quarter Horse are by his disposition and appearance of strength. Quarter Horses stand still when they're not working or competing. Most are calm horses that don't flinch or shy at strangers. The Quarter Horse gives you the idea, to look at him, that he is a powerful animal and has himself under control.

Here's how the typical Quarter Horse shapes up, from nose to tail:

Head

The Quarter Horse's head is a bit shorter than heads of most other breeds. He has small "fox ears." His cheeks and jaws are

"... cheeks and jaws are full ... eyes set wide apart ..."

full and big. Because the head is broad, a Quarter Horse's eyes are set wide apart. The nostrils are big and the jaws well-developed.

Neck

The neck should meet a Quarter Horse's body at about a 45 degree angle. This is a lot different from some of the Eastern breeds where horses are bred and trained to keep their heads up in the air. The good Quarter Horse keeps his head down where he can use it and the rider can see over it. His neck will be of medium length and will blend well into the shoulder.

Fore Quarters

The shoulders will slope down at about 45 degrees. (You get on a horse with steep shoulders that go straight down and you'll feel like you were riding a car with one flat tire. It'll be rough.)

The Quarter Horse will have a deep, wide chest so there's

a big, healthy "V" space between his forelegs. The forearms—where his front legs meet his body—will have plenty of muscle inside and out.

The withers on a good Quarter Horse will be easy to see. That's the ridge of bone and muscle where his neck meets his back—and it's what keeps the saddle on when he stops quick. The withers will be as high, or maybe a little higher, than the croup.

Some years ago there was a type of Quarter Horse called the "bulldog" type. This was a stock horse with too *much* muscle in front, and "mutton" withers. Riders complained they couldn't keep their saddles on them and one saddlery said that building a saddletree for a bulldog type was sort of like trying to make a saddle to fit a barrel.

You can see why the bulldog type is not very popular anymore.

Back

Lots of Quarter Horses must carry over 250 pounds of rider and saddle, so the back and loin have to be short-coupled and well-muscled. The middle shouldn't be paunchy. (That would keep him from turning fast.) The underline of the horse will come straight back to the flank.

Hind Quarters

You sometimes hear it said that a good Quarter Horse will have a face like a lady and hind quarters like a cook. There's some truth to this. Nearly all good-bred Quarter Horses do have big, muscular hips and legs. This is where they get all that sudden speed, and it's what helps anchor them down for quick stops.

The Quarter Horse will have lots of width through the stifle. In fact, when you stand behind him, you shouldn't be able to see the swell of his ribs on either side. He'll have plenty of muscle on the inside and outside of the hind legs too. This is something Quarter Horse breeders pay lots of attention to. The hindquarters give Quarter Horses their power.

Breed Characteristics

Feet And Legs

The feet are medium size, the hoof is usually oblong instead of round. The hocks are set low to the ground, which makes the rear cannon bone pretty short. With lots of length *above* the hock, the Quarter Horse has the leverage he needs for fast movements.

Color

Quarter Horses come in 12 colors and shades. The breed registry won't recognize albinos, apaloosas, and paints.

You may hear lots of old-time horsemen talking about horses with colors like blue-black, chestnut-sorrel, cream, yellow and so on, but here are the official Quarter Horse colors—as they have to appear on registration papers:

Black	Chestnut (a shade of Sorrel)	Red Roan (strawberry roan)
Brown	Buckskin (black mane and tail)	Blue Roan
Bay	Red Dun (red mane and tail)	Grulla (mouse color)
Sorrel	Palomino (white mane and tail)	Gray

Some Quarter Horsemen swear that one color is better than another for their stock. I personally don't think it makes much difference. I'll go along with the Spanish. They say that you don't find a bad color on a good horse.

Stance

The thing you'll notice first about a Quarter Horse's stance is how he looks "collected." His hind feet are well under him. All four feet are usually flat on the ground. He can go in any direction in a hurry. Notice how all four legs come straight down from his body.

Movements

The Quarter Horse moves with a smooth, straight stride. He doesn't skim his feet along just above the ground and he doesn't pick them up high. They're picked up freely and put down flat on the ground.

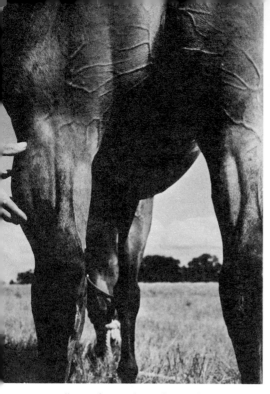

". . . plenty of muscle on the inside and outside of the hind legs . . ."

"The hocks are set low to the ground . . ."

In a lope, the Quarter Horse looks relaxed and runs easy. He has to be able to speed up, stop, back up, or pivot right now. The good Quarter Horse responds to a squeeze of a rider's knees or the touch of a rein. He should never need any great pressure on the bit to obey.

Most trained Quarter Horses will work well or compete with only a rope around their necks.

Registration

One of the complicated things about the Quarter Horse breed is the different levels of breeding registration.

All Quarter Horses aren't the same quality. The better ancestors he had, the better your horse probably is. To give Quarter Horses credit for good bloodlines and yet still recognize good Quarter Horses with only fair ancestors—that's the problem.

The Quarter Horse breed solves it with three levels of breeding—the Permanent, Tentative, and the Appendix registries—

and a set-up by which a horse earns points in performance contests, halter shows, by producing high-quality colts, and passing inspections. By his ability, that is, he can climb up "through the ranks."

The Quarter Horse inspection program is one that has a lot of time, money, and manpower in it. At the last count there were eight full-time inspectors going all over the country inspecting Quarter Horses for registration or for advancement to a higher registry.

This table gives an idea of how much work this takes and how strict those inspectors must be to make sure horses measure up on conformation, color, and breeding before they're passed.

American Quarter Horse Inspections

Year	Miles driven by inspectors	Horses assigned for inspection	Accepted	Rejected
1957	264,890	9,007	70%	30%
1956	199,011	5,888	68%	32%

And there's a lot more to this inspection and registration business. To figure out the breeding and qualification charts, you have to remember that the American Quarter Horse Association, as it is now, takes in a couple of other groups. It was reorganized in 1950 to include the American Quarter Running Association and the National Quarter Horse Breeders Association.

The horses listed in those two groups were included into the new AQHA registration program.

That's why anybody who figures to do any Quarter Horse breeding better plan on spending some time studying the publications put out by the AQHA on registration.

There are two booklets that every Quarter Horse owner should read and keep on hand. One is the AQHA Show And Contest Handbook. The other is the official handbook entitled "Bylaws and Registrations, Rules and Regulations." You can get them free of charge by writing to The American Quarter Horse Association, 2736 West Tenth Ave., P. O. Box 271, Amarillo, Texas.

2 HOW THE BREED DEVELOPED

The American Quarter Horse has been an official breed only since 1940. That was the year the American Quarter Horse Association was organized and registration started for horses that met the breed standards.

But the history of the Quarter Horse goes back a long way —back before the time when anybody kept good accounts of what stock horses in this country even looked like.

The first records that say anything about "Quarter" horses were put down by Colonial writers who saw stocky little ponies used for both work and sport.

They'd be plowhorses or transportation during the week, and on weekends they'd be raced along trails in the woods or through the village streets. Sometimes they'd have so many races in a village that two groups of horses would be started at opposite ends of the street and they'd pass each other at the half-way mark. I'll bet that must have been pretty wild.

Some of the experts who've studied early records think most of these horses, used between 1650 and 1750, had Spanish ancestors. The early English settlers did bring work horses over with them before 1620, but not many. The woods of Florida were already full of wild horses that had gotten away, or been stolen, from the early Spanish settlements.

The Spaniards had started sending horses over this way with Columbus. There were stock farms in the West Indies before 1600 and it didn't take long for the Indians to separate the Spaniards from some of the horses brought to Florida.

After the English and the Indians started raiding the Spanish towns of Florida and the Carolinas, wild horses spread north. It got to be a regular sport among the colonial settlers to try and capture them. *

A "breed" mentioned by some early writers of this period was the Chickasaw pony, named after the Chickasaw Indians who rode a stocky little horse that got to be popular for short races.

Of course, those early settlers didn't need horses just to race. They had all they could do to raise crops and stay alive. But it was good entertainment and also a way to breed better horses. When some village turned up a stallion with lots of speed, he'd be in demand for breeding.

All this happened before there was any such thing as a Thoroughbred race horse. They came along in the 18th century. One of the first in this country was a horse called Janus.

He was brought from England about 1752 and from what's been written about Janus he was quite a sire. A compact horse, Janus was supposed to have been a short-racing type of Thoroughbred with more speed than distance ability. Most Quarter Horse pedigrees trace back to Janus, one way or another.

You get the idea that he must have been bred to just about every mare in the colonies.

---

*   The Horse of the Americas by Robert M. Denhardt, pages 179-180

Races then were short and simple contests. Usually it was a match between two horses. This was before anyone had built any circular tracks in this country and the race distance was about a quarter of a mile. They recognized the good horses with titles like "Famous American Quarter Running Horse," or "Celebrated American Quarter Running Mare."

John H. Wallace in his book "The Horse of America" quotes a man named J. F. D. Smith, who toured the colonies before the Revolutionary War, as saying this:

> "In the southern part of the colony and in N. C., they are much attached to Quarter Racing, which is always a match between two horses to run one quarter of a mile, straight out, being merely an exertion of speed; and they have a breed that performs it with an astonishing velocity . . . . ."

When the English Thoroughbred got well established after the Revolutionary War, interest in short races dropped off. They started building longer, Thoroughbred tracks and the horse races eventually got up to four miles long. The fast, short-legged ponies still raced when they weren't being used for work—but the big money and breeding were going into Thoroughbreds.

All this time, there was another part of the country where "short" horses were being bred—but not on purpose. In the Southwest—where Texas is now—wild Spanish Mustangs were still running loose. They were first cousins to those early Chickasaw ponies and they were just as sturdy and fast as the best of them.

That's why the first cattlemen in Texas didn't have to worry about where their cow ponies were coming from. The horses were there when the cowmen arrived. These Southwest Mustangs, like the Southeast Chickasaws, grew from ponies stolen from or lost by the Spanish missions and explorers.

And a tougher breed of horse probably never lived. The Mustang could get along on brush and scrub grass and almost no water. There wasn't much they were afraid of because they were almost wild animals themselves.

Once caught and broke to the saddle, they made good cow horses. They could work and keep going as long as any man they carried.

But even before the Civil War, cattlemen wanted to cross the Mustang with a longer-legged horse, to give them more speed so they could cover more ground. And so the Thoroughbred came to the Southwest.

Some of the first were shipped by water to Galveston from New Orleans in 1839. The breeder was the most famous Texan of them all, Sam Houston. He was President of the new Republic of Texas then, and a man who knew a good utility horse when he saw one.

One of his stallions, named Copperbottom, is almost as familiar a name in the Texas horse world as Sam Houston's name is in the state's history books. Nobody knows for sure how many Quarter-type horses Copperbottom and the two other stallions produced, but in the Houston-Galveston area they were still talking about "Copperbottom" horses when the 20th century started. He produced colts that stood about 14½ hands high, had small ears set wide apart, wide forehead, big eyes, heavy-muscled jaws, arched ribs and well-muscled hind-quarters. * They were much in demand for work and for short races.

But the two things didn't always mix. Some cattlemen who bred good horses felt like too much racing would ruin a horse for cow work. Of course, now and then they'd race their best horses against their neighbor's—which is one reason why every rancher was always on the lookout for faster horses to use for breeding purposes. Sometimes it was a matter of family honor to have a horse you could match against any that came along.

Another of the early horses supposed to have added much to the Quarter Horse breed was Steel Dust. He's probably had more

---

* "Pioneer Thoroughbreds and Quarter Horses in Texas" by Leon van Meldert in The Western Horseman Magazine, Jan.-Feb., 1942.

stories told about him than any of the early short racing horses. He was foaled in 1849 and, by all accounts, was about the fastest "short" horse of his time.

So much of a reputation did Steel Dust get that, pretty soon, he began siring colts in places he'd never been. In fact, up until recent years, lots of cowmen would refer to a Quarter-type horse as a "steel dust."

One writer, Robert Denhart, wrote that "Every horse trader who has not recently joined a church will modestly admit that his horses are direct descendants of Steel Dust." *

One of the interesting things about some of the famous early horses is the names they were given. If you didn't know, you'd think they were all people.

It wasn't unusual in those days—and even yet—to name Quarter Horses after some friend of yours, or even yourself.

That's why the oldtimers would call off names like A. D. Reed, Alice Wood, Buck Thomas, John Wilkens, Lou Trammel, Roger Mills, Bessie Keough, Dollie Spokes, Harmon Baker, and Peter McCue—and then have to say whether they meant the person or the horse.

The last horse named, Peter McCue, may yet turn out to be the best-known Quarter Horse in history. He was registered as a Thoroughbred—although he sure didn't *run* like one—but later got most of his reputation in short races.

His owners sort of suspected Peter McCue wasn't much of a distance racer in 1898, when he finished first only once in ten starts—and his only win was in a ⅝ mile race, against four horses, with him carrying only 90 pounds. Later, this horse won a lot of short races in Colorado, Oklahoma, Texas and Missouri, and is considered one of the two most prominent sires of the Quarter Horse breed.**

There have been a lot of famous cattle ranches in Texas history that did plenty to improve the cowhorse. I won't try and list

---

* The Quarter Horse—A History, The American Quarter Horse Association, Stud Book and Registry, Vol. I, 1941, p. 18.
** Journal of Heredity, J. Lane Fletcher, pp 346-352.

"Peter McCue may yet turn out to be the best-known Quarter Horse in history."

them all here, but after the Civil War the breeding of better range ponies was something everybody in the cow business worked at.

Some of the earliest and best-kept records were those of Captain Richard King who founded the King Ranch. He wrote that he went to Kentucky in 1868 to buy "blood stallions to improve my horse herd." *

King had started trying to build a better cow horse some years before that. He had picked out the best Mustangs on his place for breeding and had split up the mares into color groups.

With those "blood stallions," he started producing cow ponies almost 15 hands high. They were so much better than most other stock horses that horse thieves from all over Texas tried to figure a way to make off with a King Ranch horse. Some did. Some tried to, got caught and got hanged.

In the 1880's the King Ranch people were still trying to get

* The King Ranch, Tom Lea, Appendix XIV, p. 732

just exactly the kind of cow horse they wanted. They shipped in some Thoroughbreds, Standardbreds and a few Arabians and Morgan Horse sires.

The first and second crosses on Spanish mares produced good horses all right and in some years the ranch sold more horses than cattle. But they didn't breed true to one single type, generation after generation. *

It wasn't until 1916 that the King Ranch started the line of horses it's known for today.

Robert J. Kleberg, Jr., who runs the ranch today, then saw a colt at cattleman George Clegg's place near Alice, Texas. He got his cousin, Caesar Kleberg, to buy it for the ranch. This colt became "Old Sorrel"—the foundation sire for nearly all later King Ranch Quarter Horses.

When a group of cattlemen got together and formed the American Quarter Horse Association in 1940, and set up a breed registry, horse number one in that registry was Wimpy, a grandson of Old Sorrel.

What happened to the Quarter Horse in the years between 1840 and 1940 is something not all Quarter Horse breeders agree on. Most of them do agree that crossing Thoroughbred stallions onto Spanish Mustang mares had a lot to do with getting the kind of Quarter Horse we have now.

But there's no one horse and no one group of horses you can point to and say: "There's right where the Quarter Horse started." It was something that happened in a lot of places, on a lot of ranches, in the space of maybe 75 years. Different cattlemen probably had different ideas on just what their "dream" horses should look like. They sure didn't all use the same breeding programs to get it.

But they all knew they needed a horse that could do a lot of things well, one that was smart and good-natured, had quick speed and cow sense. They bred toward these things by keeping horses with those qualities, and getting rid of those without them.

---

* The King Ranch, By Tom Lea, Appendix XIV, p. 733

3 HOW QUARTER HORSES ARE USED

You can divide the way Quarter Horses are used into about six general classes.

They are farm and ranch work horses and they're used for Quarter Horse performance contests, rodeos, halter shows, and straightaway racing. That's five. A sixth use would take in all the odd jobs people do on horseback these days: trail riding, parades, polo, jumping, cutter racing on the snow, horseback square dancing—the list can get pretty long if you put in everything.

To know Quarter Horses you should have an idea of what the breed does in each of these divisions.

Farm and Ranch Work

Quarter Horse people agree that as much as half of all this breed are still used at what the animal was bred for—working livestock. But you can't pick a figure and say that's the number of Quarter Horses on ranches alone, since nearly all good ranch ponies do something *else* nowadays besides work.

A lot of them are used in weekend rodeos. Others that have their registration papers in shape are entered in performance contests. Quite a few are good enough to enter halter shows. You can probably find some ranch horses that are used for everything a Quarter Horse does—and they do more different things, as a breed, than any other kind of horse in the world.

Now I don't mean to say that *every* ranch horse in America is a Quarter Horse. When I talk about Quarter Horses I mean those that have American Quarter Horse Association registration papers. But nearly all ranch horses are of the Quarter Horse *type*—that is, they're calm, agile, stocky ponies with lots of "early speed"—the kind you need to catch and manage livestock.

Just about every rancher would like to have nothing but registered Quarter Horses on his place and lots of them have started their own breeding programs. They'll buy a good Quarter Horse stallion and a few mares and start up-grading their riding stock. Good horses can make a lot of difference in ranch work too. Not only do Quarter Horses learn faster and work better than poor-bred horses, but they make the work more pleasant.

There's nothing easy about honest-to-goodness ranching. And most cattlemen figure that as long as they've got to spend lots of time in a saddle, they may as well have the best horses under them they can get.

You may have liked your old Model-T once upon a time, but when better-made cars came along, you bought them.

Rodeos

Every year, more professional and amateur rodeo cowboys get better-bred horses. Doing this helps them win more often. It also makes for a better rodeo to the spectators.

So it's pretty certain that the growth of rodeo as a sport has had a lot to do with making Quarter Horses so popular. Just about all your best roping and bulldogging horses now are registered Quarter Horses.

I'd think the horse is one big reason so many more people go to rodeos too. Most people in this country just naturally like to see good horses and good riders compete.

When you see what kind of crowds go to just the rodeos where RCA members compete (those who belong to the Rodeo Cowboy's Association) you can tell what a popular sport it is now.

More than 13,000,000 people went to the 463 RCA shows in 1957—and the crowds are getting bigger every year.

These RCA shows, I ought to add, are the "major leagues" of rodeo. There's no telling how many small-town, county fair, high school and college rodeos are held all over the country every month. But the RCA figures that something over 25,000,000 people in this country saw at least one rodeo in 1957.

"... your best roping and bulldogging horses now are registered Quarter Horses."

Performance Contests

These contests are strictly for Quarter Horses. And it's about what the name says—a contest to find out how good your horse performs different jobs.

There are seven events in performance contests: Roping, Cutting, Reining, Barrel Racing, Western Riding and the Working Cowhorse competition are the ones you see at most Quarter Horse shows. The other one, Straightaway Racing, has a different way of being judged and it's held on a race track.

The idea behind performance contests is to help improve the Quarter Horse breed. That's why only registered Quarter Horses can compete. As you can see, all the events have come from the old-time ranching skills.

The whole idea has grown up since 1950. Before that, the only performance event was straightaway racing. Starting about 1953, Quarter Horse shows were organized almost every time some new state association was formed. There were 90 shows in 1953. In 1957 there were 354 shows in 33 states, which means that Quarter Horse shows are pretty big business now.

I think one reason they've gotten so popular is that lots of people, no matter what their age, want to compete on horseback —especially if they have good-bred horses. Until the Quarter Horse show came along there was no sort of big western show they could enter. Most business people, of course, don't have the time to enter rodeos.

The performance events give everybody with Quarter Horses something to shoot at. There's half a dozen events to enter and sometimes, with a good horse, you can win in two or three.

Then, along with ribbons, trophies and small purses, you can earn "points." You get so many points for winning first, second, third, and so on—how many points you get depends on how many horses are entered in the event.

These points help you get your horse listed in the yearly Quarter Horse "Register of Merit." They also help him qualify for the top honor a Quarter Horse can win—the AQHA Champion Award.

Halter Shows

Here's another use for the Quarter Horse that's popular with folks who've gotten interested in the breed. This event is not to test your horse's performance—only how well he's built.

There are some horses, like I said earlier, that can do good in both the performance end of Quarter Horse competition and also in the halter shows. But most breeders feel that while the halter show is a good thing, all Quarter Horses should prove themselves as "using" horses too if they're going to be worth anything. I think that if they're good enough to work, they're good enough to show. I don't believe in just feeding and leading a horse.

In other words, contests for beauty and conformation are fine —as long as the horse can still do the things he was bred to do.

From the horse owner's standpoint, halter shows give you a good place to compare your pony with others. You learn a lot about the breed and if you show a mare or stallion, those winner's ribbons improve the price you can ask for colts out of those animals later on.

Straightaway Racing

There was a time in the last century, after the Civil War, when Quarter Horse racing in the Southwest was something that happened everywhere, most all the time. But they didn't call it that then, and there was nothing fancy about it. The people of a town just got together in some big open space to watch—and bet on—any ranch ponies that the cowboys or ranch owners wanted to run.

A lot of money changed hands in those days and there were famous horses that made big reputations for themselves. But "short races" dropped off in the first half of this century. Automobiles, I think, had a lot to do with it.

"... if they're good enough to work, they're good enough to show."

It wasn't until after the Quarter Horse breed association was started in 1940 that the short races got popular again. Beginning about 1948—mostly in Arizona and California—Quarter racing came back.

The table will show how it has grown since 1954.

	1957	1956	1955	1954
Total race meets	37	30	33	32
Total purses	$ 1,471,633	1,321,667	1,125,498	900,933
Average purse	$ 933	876	844	693
Total handle	$34,019,632	31,106,871	25,603,345	18,950,703
No. of races	1,671	1,509	1,333	1,300

Some good Quarter running horses are used both on ranches and for work. But most owners and trainers don't think you can expect to win much racing money with the average ranch, rodeo, or performance contest Quarter Horse.

The serious racing breeders usually pick Quarter Horses for training that have some recent Thoroughbred blood in them. This gives extra speed at the short distances.

How Quarter Horses Are Used

But if a breeder is not careful, he can start producing horses that don't have the muscle and "action" to handle livestock too.

Miscellaneous

About 1934, I was breaking some horses for a man at Lamesa, Texas. His horses were all Quarter Horse-type ponies, although this was before the breed association was formed and we didn't call them that.

Anyway, some of his friends had been kidding him about his stocky, little horses compared to their own long-legged Thoroughbred horses, so they set up a polo game and asked my boss to play.

But he got sick before the game and they decided to put me in there in his place. I kind of dreaded this because I didn't know whether they'd hit the ball, or hit me, with those sticks.

Some of the other riders made fun of the little horse I was riding that day. He was from a famous Quarter stallion named Joe Reed and I knew he could run. But he did look different from those tall Thoroughbreds, with their tails all sheared like a mule. I guess they thought my bay pony would just get in the way. And he did too.

Before the match, a friend of mine took an interest in my horse and showed me how to hit the ball. He told me I could do it all right because, like roping, it was a matter of timing, speed and distance.

Anyway, the game started, they knocked the ball out there and first thing I knew we were all wadded up like we were having a convention. I still didn't know for sure what I was doing but I saw the ball and took out after it. Before they could catch me I'd knocked it through the goal.

The other riders were good sports and they got a big kick out of how that pony of mine could get around. They found out their Thoroughbreds couldn't catch my horse in less than 100 yards. He could also stop, turn and be over yonder while they wondered where he went.

I didn't make but one goal that day but I got in everybody else's way so *they* couldn't make any. Everybody who saw the game learned a lot about Quarter Horses—and I learned a lot about polo. I found out they play it seven minutes to a chukker —and that's a long time to work *that* hard at anything—even picking cotton.

Polo on Quarter Horses hasn't become as popular yet as it may someday—partly because it's a team game and solo competition on horseback is still what most riders seem to like best right now. But there are places in Arizona and California where "indoor" arenas have been built for miniature polo. These arenas actually are outdoors and are about one-third as big as the 150 by 300-yard polo fields in the East. There are three men and horses to a team in this small polo game, instead of the four-man teams of Eastern polo. It's a faster game too—there aren't many long runs or hits made in a 100-yard arena. It's mostly short hits, quick turns and lots of speed. This has been played with Quarter Horses for several years in the Tuscon area, especially.

Here are other ways Quarter Horsemen are using their mounts for sport and pleasure:

In states like Wyoming and Utah, Quarter Horses are being hitched as teams, to sleds, and raced through the snow. They call it cutter racing.

At a few Eastern horse shows, Quarter Horses are used as jumpers.

In the Southwest, some towns have what's called pole-bending races. This event calls for the horse and rider to weave in and out through a line of eight, upright poles. It's a tough event because it doesn't really give the horse a chance to change leads before he has to change back again. It's a good test of both horse and rider.

Also in Texas, an event that's lots of fun to watch, as well as ride in, is Palmetto Polo. This is sort of a poor-boy version of full-size polo. It's played with a big rubber ball and rubber-tipped mallets. There are five players on a team and it's often played in arenas as small as 40 yards wide and 80 yards long. I read recently where more than 50 Palmetto Polo teams had been organized in Texas and looked like something else that youngsters could enjoy as a Quarter Horse sport.

There's one thing I haven't mentioned yet that's being done with lots of Quarter Horses. That's pleasure riding alone. Here again you can't pick a figure on how many of the breed are kept for nothing *but* this, but state and regional Quarter Horse associations now are all over the country. They're made up of pleasure horsemen mostly. They get together for shows, sometimes contests and always lots of horse-talk about breeding and training.

I suppose one of the biggest of these get-togethers happens in February every year around Houston. To open their Fat Stock show, trail riders come in to town from three directions. On the

"People who've never seen this are usually pretty surprised."

biggest of these, the Salt Grass Trail ride, you can find more than 1,000 horses, riders, and chuck wagons coming down through the countryside together.

People who've never seen this are usually pretty surprised. Couple of years back the trail ride was crossing a highway and traffic was tied up for quite awhile. One woman motorist from another part of the country saw all those riders stretched out for a mile or more and she wanted to know what it was all about.

When she got out of her car and asked one of the riders, he took off his hat and looked down.

"A cowboy just died, ma'am. This is his funeral."

After you've read this book, you'll have a good idea why the average Quarter Horse owner gets to be pretty crazy about his horse and his breed. I think the big reason is easy to understand.

The old-time cattlemen who improved the cowpony and helped start the Quarter Horse breed wanted a horse that was good to ride, sturdy, smart and easy to live with. They didn't go for foolish, high-strung horses or ones they weren't comfortable on.

Their work is paying off for all of us who use this breed today.

4 BUYING THE QUARTER HORSE

In Calvert, Texas, in 1940, I was buying quite a few horses. I'd buy them, train them, and then sell them. My neighbors all knew it and they'd often show me horses they'd want to sell.

One day at an auction in Calvert, a man came up wanting to sell me a pretty little dapple, iron gray mare, for $40.

He said he'd guarantee the horse to be broke gentle enough for a kid to ride. (He never did say *whose* kid.) He also said the horse had been used plenty under a saddle. So I bought the horse and took her out in an alley behind the barn to saddle her up.

She had no sense at all. Almost went crazy when I put that saddle on her. But I got her saddled and managed to ride her enough to make her sweat. Then I got my shears and trimmed her tail and cut off her mane. She looked pretty good, so I figured I'd have some fun with the fellow who sold her to me.

I put her in the auction ring that afternoon and waited outside.

Sure enough, this same man I'd bought the horse from, bid on her and bought her back for $75. A little later he came up and said to me: "Say, I want to sell you a pony to match that one you bought this morning." And he took me over to that same little mare.

"You can tell she's been ridden a lot," he told me.

"That's right," I told him. "I rode her some this morning—right after I bought her from you."

After a minute he laughed. "Let's go get a drink—they're on me," he said.

This is the kind of thing that's always made people cautious about buying horses. In years gone by you didn't know for sure what a horse's breeding was or what you were getting—unless you were in the business yourself. And then you didn't *always* know.

But times have changed. Quarter Horse auction sales are run by some strict rules. Horse pedigrees have to be shown and there's plenty of chance to find out what kind of training a horse has *really* had. Also, the Quarter Horse breeders don't like to sell any horses that don't measure up to the reputations they've built for their string of horses.

Which means that buyers now are pretty sure to get their money's worth—if they do a little thinking beforehand about what they want from a horse and how they're going to use him. It doesn't hurt to know how an auction works, either—so those are some things we'll talk about in this chapter.

Cost Of Maintenance

Keeping a Quarter Horse is not much different than keeping any other breed. Except you don't need a ranch, as some may think. Lots of horsemen have less than an acre of land. But you would want to have some space near you—if you don't own farm property—to exercise your horse.

You can figure to spend $15 to $20 a month to feed your

horse, depending on the time of year and where you live. Once in awhile, you'll spend a few dollars on a veterinarian to give your pony shots or see to him when he doesn't feel like he ought to. Of course, you'll need saddle and bridle, and every couple of months you'll need to spend money for new horseshoes, if you give your horse the exercise you should.

Which means we're talking about roughly $250 a year to feed him and keep him healthy.

What Sex To Buy

There's some other things you want to think about too when you go to buy your horse. Like what sex to buy.

You probably don't want a stallion, unless you're figuring to breed horses later on. A stallion is all right if just one man handles him all the time. He's sure a lot more valuable if you buy a good Quarter Horse stallion as a colt and raise him yourself. But if you just want him to ride, the stallion is naturally going to be a little unpredictable in the spring and fall.

The mare makes a better pleasure horse, but there's the usual problem of her coming in heat every 18 to 21 days and in that condition she can be a little unpredictable too. A mare—like a stallion—does have breeding value for quite a few years and you can often pay for your mare pretty easy with her colts.

For pleasure horse use, I don't guess you can beat the gelding. He's been castrated and he doesn't have his mind on much of anything but eating and sleeping and doing what you want him to do.

You'll find a lot of your best rodeo and contest ponies are geldings, and that's the reason. They're just a lot easier to handle. Also, because they're no good for breeding, they're less expensive than mares and stallions.

Past Training Of A Horse

Because Quarter Horses are used for lots of things, you'll find many that are well-trained in both stock-handling and show competition. Some of these trained ponies make good pleasure horses and some don't. You want to ask around before you buy one and give some thought to how that horse might fit you or your family, and your experience.

I'm sometimes asked if roping or cutting horses make good pleasure horses.

I don't much think you'd want a roping horse for pleasure riding only. You have to remember the horse was taught to catch livestock. So if you were riding along and came across a cow, the horse might do what he was trained to do—and you'd better be prepared for it if you're just learning.

Matter of fact, a trained roping horse doesn't always make a good cow horse either, once he's out of competition. I've had roping horses I couldn't work cattle on in a pasture—that I could hardly pen cattle on at all.

If a cow runs off and you want to "head" her, the roping horse doesn't want to go around her—he just wants to catch her. He's been trained to stay behind.

Now the trained cutting horse might make a better pleasure horse but you'd want to be a better than fair rider.

This pony can just about duck right out from under you, if he's a good cutting horse. You might be loping along, go to rein him over, and put a little too much pressure on the rein. He can be turned all the way around, headed the other direction, before you know it. A cutting horse is kind of like an automobile. He's geared to go.

But if you know what kind of horse he is, and you can handle him all right, you might be spoiled for good. After having a horse that sensitive on the reins you'd probably figure all other horses after him were pretty dumb or else awful slow.

That's the thing lots of horsemen like about horses trained for cutting. When you want that horse to move over, just touch the reins. He doesn't go way down the trail to move over. He moves right *there.*

Buying The Quarter Horse

Buying Direct From A Breeder

Let's say you've decided to buy a Quarter Horse for pleasure riding and you go to a man who breeds and raises them for sale. It's not hard to find Quarter Horse breeders in any part of the country. They're usually pretty well-known horsemen. They also advertise in the horse, cattle or farm magazines.

Anyway, there's some things you want to know about any horse or colt you may buy. You want to ask—as I said a ways back—what this horse has been trained for up to now. You want to know if he's been roped off of much, if he's worked cattle, if he's a quiet horse. Naturally, you want to know his age and you'll see this when you look at the registration papers.

You want to ask about any illnesses the horse has had. If you ride him hard will be get sore across his kidneys? Get on the horse and you may be able to tell that. If he's sore over his loins, he'll go down in his back some when you mount. This could be serious.

Another thing—has the horse been spoiled? Are there things that he won't do? How's his breathing—is it steady and regular? If not, it might mean he's been used too hard and had his wind broke.

You also want to know if he's been hauled much in a trailer, if he's been in town or out around people very much.

When you pick out your riding pony from some man's herd be sure to ride the horse and see if he's what you want. This is the best thing you can do since you have a chance to get the feel of the horse. You can tell a lot about how he reins. You can see if he's a barn crazy horse that wants to turn and run for the barn the minute you head off across the pasture, and if he lets you give the orders or tries to tell you where *he* wants to go.

And you sure want to check up on the horse's breeding. Even if he's a gelding, you may sometime want to show the horse in halter competition. So check the registration papers and make sure of the horse's sire and dam.

"there's some things you want to know about any horse or colt you may buy."

Buying At Auction

Like lots of other things, a horse is worth what somebody will pay to own him. That's why the public auction is a good place to find out what Quarter Horse prices are like.

At an auction you have the same chance to look the horses over that every other buyer has. The top bid fixes a horse's market value, and that's why horse magazines like *The Quarter Horse Journal, Western Horsemen* and *Horse Lovers* run stories about auctions. You might say that the auction is to the horse business what the stock market is to the investment business.

If you saw those average auction prices in the Introduction, you've already decided that good Quarter Horses don't come cheap. This is true. But a lot depends on what you want a horse for.

A nice gelding for pleasure riding only can be found for less than $500 at many of the Quarter Horse auctions. It might be smart, though, to pay an extra $300 for a horse if you find one that's had some training. It'll be worth the money.

If, on the other hand, you want a pony that'll help you win some cutting or barrel racing contests, you ought to figure on spending from $900 up. I think a person would be smart to go to a couple of auctions, look at the horses as they're sold, find out what they can do, then decide about what you want to pay. You may want to go to two or three sales before you buy.

Quarter Horse breeders are mighty careful about their reputations. They'd rather give a young horse away than to sell him to a person who'd be dissatisfied later on.

If you figure to buy at an auction, it's a good idea to get there ahead of time and look at all the horses to be sold.

There will be catalogues handy with the pictures and the bloodlines (the breeding) of all the horses in that sale. But you still need to see those horses yourself.

Once in awhile, at sales, you can find the men who raised them or trained them. This is good because they'll tell you about any horse and they'll tell you right.

If a cowboy or trainer tells you a horse is a little bit spooky, he *is* a little bit spooky. If he tells you a horse has a good mouth, and cow sense, then he has it. This is because when you work all day, week after week, with a horse—well, you sure don't brag on him if he doesn't rate it.

In other words, if he's a lazy horse or there's something wrong with him, you soon come to think of him like you would a mooching man. You have no use for him. He's just a star boarder.

So if you find the man who raised a horse, you can find out real fast what a horse is like and what he can, or can't, do.

The auction people don't mind you looking all the stock over. Fact is, they want you to. The experienced horseman will get there ahead of time and spend hours looking around and asking questions.

". . . bid takers in the ring will see your signal and call out your bid."

But you'll be told about any serious defects a horse has when the auction starts. The auctioneers and the men who help him see to it that a horse's good and bad points are called to everybody's attention. When the horse goes into the auction ring for bidding, the auctioneer is expected to point to any defect—like a scar on the horse's ankle or a speck in his eye.

A man called the "starter" helps the auctioneer know about these things. It's also his job to set a base price on the horse—the place where the bidding starts. Naturally, he doesn't start it by "setting the hair on one," either. Meaning that if he thinks the horse may bring $1,000, he'll start the bidding at maybe half that price so more bidders will have a chance.

The auctioneer will have three or four men in the ring watching the crowd for bids. All you have to do to bid is hold your hand up. If you're not familiar with auctions, you won't have much luck understanding what the auctioneer says. He talks fast, like auctioneers do, but you'll get the drift of what the bid is pretty easy.

Buying The Quarter Horse

If you decide to bid on a horse the bid takers in the ring will see your signal and call out your bid. Then if somebody else bids higher, one of them will point at you to give you a chance to up your bid. If you want to, just give him a nod and he won't point at you again unless somebody raises your bid. If you still have the bid when the auctioneer quits, you've bought the horse.

You're expected to pay by check or cash when the sale is over, and before you load your horse.

If you want to pick your horse up next day, the people putting on the sale usually have places where you can leave the horse overnight and come back with a trailer later on.

Smaller Auctions

In most western states you'll find country horse sales and auctions where the stock is mostly "cold-blooded," common horses. A man will gather up the ponies he doesn't need, bring them to town and sell them at the auction. Sometimes the auctioneers may tell you they're "kid broke." I sometimes wonder if there's enough kids to break all the horses that are kid broke.

You'll find some of these horses that may look a little bit like a Quarter Horse—and they may call them that. Maybe they do have some Quarter Horse blood in them, back a ways. But it's so far back, usually, it'll never catch up.

People who sell these horses we usually call "jockeys." That's another name for a horse trader. If he can make $10 on a horse, he'll trade with you—some way.

You're not apt to find good Quarter Horses at many of the smaller country sales. These are the sales that do supply lots of horses for riding stables, though, and they're not all bad ponies. But some are "soapers." They're half knocked out, their legs are boogered up, they're pretty old and they're just about ready to be made into soap or dogmeat.

At this kind of auction, too, you can get fooled pretty bad on a baby colt if you're not careful.

Most all colts, when they're four or five months old, are just awful pretty. Until they get older you may not know exactly what you've bought. If you can study a horse as a two-year-old, though, you can tell just about what he'll look like when he's six.

Anyway, if a man wants a Quarter Horse, I wouldn't advise him to go someplace where they *might* have some Quarter Horses. Once you've seen both kinds of auctions, you'll know what I mean.

Ethics Of The Business

You get a bunch of Quarter Horse people together and you'd think you had a big family reunion. Everybody knows most everybody else and they're friendly. These people aren't jealous of so-and-so because he owns this horse or that one, and they trust each other.

If a Quarter Horse man sends you to some breeder to buy a special horse, you can be plenty sure that horse is going to be just the way you were told he'd be. About the worst thing that anybody can do is to try and misrepresent a horse—and any good breeder won't sell some horses just for that reason.

Naturally, not all Quarter Horses are perfect—maybe they've got some physical defect or maybe they're just born about half mad. That's why you see so many cowboys riding Quarter Horses in rodeos. Every year some breeders give a few problem horses away. The cowboy, who's a professional, spends lots of time making something out of a horse that maybe nobody else could do a thing with. And the horse may turn into a good dogging, roping or even cutting horse.

Of course, breeders give some horses away for other reasons too.

It's one of the best ways they've found to advertise their stock —especially at high school rodeos, where a breeder may put up a good Quarter Horse colt as a prize.

You give a kid a pony and he'll tell *everybody*. And he'll *write* the ones he don't know!

". . . when you first saddle him up, he can be a little stiff and cold."

5 OWNING THE QUARTER HORSE

No matter what kind of animals you own, if you own them very long, you have to figure out how to get along with them. Not everybody does this the same way.

I remember one fellow I knew once who trained six full-grown Brahman bulls to waltz in a circle. A lot of cattlemen may think that's just not possible. But I saw them do it, and naturally I asked the man how in the world he'd trained them.

"Didn't it take an awful lot of patience?" I said.

"No," he said. "It took a lot of time and rawhide and no patience at all."

Now I don't recommend anybody using that sort of approach on a horse. But the point is—that fellow had found out what he had to do to get those bulls doing what he wanted.

And if you get anything out of a horse, *you* have to also make some effort. (Although not with rawhide!)

Just because you bought a registered Quarter Horse doesn't mean that he'll do what you want every time. He may be trained but you still have to help him understand what *you* want. Getting a good bred horse was the first step. To live with your horse, enjoy him and maybe win with him (at anything) means you have to understand him. And learn how to take proper care of him.

Maybe this sounds simple but you'd be surprised at how many people buy a good horse, then figure it's up to the horse to do everything right the first time—and from then on. The horse needs your help.

You might start by figuring that horses think more like people than any other animal. They're a lot like kids, I believe.

A child may like to do something today and he can do it good. But if he doesn't feel in just the right mood tomorrow, he doesn't do that thing so good. Same way with a horse.

If he's in the mood and doesn't feel bad—and if he understands what you want him to do—he'll usually try pretty hard for you. But he's not always going to be up to par, the same as you and me.

I sometimes think horses have to have a lot of patience with us people. We don't look at anything *their* way.

Let's say you're feeling real good today. You've just had a nap. You're just right. You decide to take a ride, so you go get your horse.

Well, *he* didn't have any notice at all. Maybe *you* figured to get some exercise, but that's no sign *he* wants some. He didn't plan on doing a thing, most likely. But he's got to go when you say go.

Sometimes you can let a horse know ahead of time what you've got in mind. If you get your horse and tie him out where he can see the trailer you use to haul him in, he'll know after a few trips that you're fixing to go someplace.

But the main thing is this—you can't have too much patience in everything you are ever going to do with your horse.

Don't Spoil Your Horse

Now I don't mean that you ought to let your horse move in like one of the family. Not unless you want a spoiled horse.

Some people treat a horse too much like he was a house pet. If you make over him all the time, pretty soon he'll get the idea that he's boss and he'll want to take over.

You should have the same attitude toward him as you would a child. Be gentle but be firm. Sure, it's okay to pet your horse when he does what you want. I believe in being good to a horse —just as nice as he'll stand.

But if he starts nipping at your arm or pulling on you, stepping on you or slobbering all over you, you're about to spoil him.

Make him stand back away from you. Flick him with a switch or leather thong—on the nose or chest or neck if he starts chewing on you. He'll catch on fast that you're in charge and not him.

Trailer Tips

If you ever plan to go anywhere with your horse besides down the road or across a pasture, you better learn something about hauling him. You'll most likely want to haul him home from where you bought him, anyway. And if you ever want to enter any sort of Quarter Horse competition—reining, cutting or halter shows—you'll need to think about owning a trailer.

First, you want to make sure your horse trailer is wide enough. You ought to have about 30 inches of width for one horse, twice that for two. If you need a two horse trailer and you get one too narrow, two horses can get to pushing each other pretty bad when you round a curve. And if you don't have a partition between them, they'll skin each other's feet up and step on each other's legs. There's a lot of horses crippled today from that.

Lengthwise, the trailer should have at least six and a half feet of space for the horse—from his chest to his rump.

Be sure too that your trailer has a hitch that'll hold it to your car or truck. Been some good horses killed from trailers coming loose and turning over.

Sometimes you see people pulling on horses for all they're worth, trying to get them in trailers. There's an easier way. Get a bucket with a little feed in it and let the horse have a sniff of it. Then you get in the trailer and offer it to the horse. He'll stick his head and neck in after the feed. Let him eat a little.

Then move the feed to the front of the trailer, getting him more into it as you go. If a horse has never been loaded in a trailer before, you may have to put one of his front feet up on the ramp to give him the idea.

In about five or 10 minutes, if you don't hurry him, the horse will want that feed bad enough to get in the trailer after it. Most modern trailers have a little door in the front where you can step out.

For trips, it's pretty important that you teach a horse to eat out of a bucket and, more especially, drink out of a bucket. This is so you can find good drinking water and carry it to him if you need to. You want to be careful about that. Even good horsemen sometimes get careless and let their horses drink just anywhere. Horses can sure catch distemper from the wrong water. Teach him to drink from a bucket at home and he'll do it anywhere you're a little wary of ponds or cisterns.

Don't get excited the first time you see a horse what we call "trailer drunk." When you unload your horse, he may stagger a little. Kind of like a man who's seasick. It won't last long, though.

Traveling With A Horse

Here's some other things to think about on trips:

Take along medicine. I like to have some Spohn's (distemper cure for colds) and Absorbine, to rub on a horse's legs. Also some kind of mild liniment.

As for feed, it's not a good idea to change feed on your horse on a trip. Whatever you feed him at home, try to feed him away from home. Changing it—especially if you make any hard runs on your horse—can cause him to be sick.

Give the horse some rest outside the trailer while you're traveling. When I stop for lunch at noon, I make sure to unload the horse and water him. And I leave him unloaded until I get ready to go again. In some places—even where the water is good —you'll find your horse won't touch it. May be too much salt or minerals in it to suit him. Don't worry too much. He may not drink for a day or two. I've seen a horse go a couple of days and not drink over a gallon of water. Remember that you've been places where you didn't much like the water yourself.

If the horse won't drink after two days though, you may want to put a little salt in his feed to make him drink some.

When you put your horse in a strange stall away from home, be sure to put him so he can't get out—and so that some other horse can't get to him. Be sure to have plenty of bedding—oat straw—for him to lay down on. If there's only hard ground underfoot he may skin himself up wallowing in a stall where there's no hay.

Of course, some horses will eat that bedding. If it's good hay it won't hurt him. But he'll probably be so full he can't run.

To keep him from eating too much hay, you might have to tie his head up for half a day—especially if you're going to enter him in some contest where you want to run that night.

He's kind of like a cowboy that way. If he can get anything to eat, he'll eat it. And he'd be better off if he wasn't so full.

Friendship With Feed

Showing a horse that you're important to him is pretty easy with his feed and water. And I've made friends with lots of horses by a couple of days of giving him very little of both.

If your horse is trained and well-gentled, you wouldn't want to do this. But say your horse is not that way when you get him.

Let's say that he came from an owner who had raised him but never handled him much. Maybe he's not even halter broke.

You can take a horse like this home and tie him to the limb of a tree about 150 to 200 yards away from any house, barn or other horses. Tie him to a stout limb that will spring a little but won't let him break loose. Let's say you tie him there at noon, after you've fed him. Leave him there without any more feed or water for 24 hours—until noon the next day.

During that time make sure nobody goes near the horse. Leave him strictly alone—if the weather is mild, of course.

After 24 hours, I've never gone back to one yet that didn't nicker when I came up. He's glad to see you after all that time.

He'll be more so when he sees you with two buckets—one with oats and one with water. He may be a little afraid to drink at first, but don't give him any water until he drinks out of the bucket. And don't give him any feed until he first eats a little grain out of your hand.

Let him eat and drink then, and when he's finished go away and leave him another 24 hours.

Two days of this and that horse is your friend. He realizes that he needs help. He remembers you brought it.

He'll be your friend and he'll believe in you from there on, if you don't abuse him. What's more, no matter how excited he may have been when you tied him to that tree, you won't have any trouble untieing him and leading him away. He's ready to go somewhere else. He's been in *that* place long enough!

Feeding Times and Habits

I like to feed an unbroke horse for a few weeks three times a day—at about 6 AM, 12 noon, and 5 PM. Feed him according to what he weighs. A gallon of grain three times a day will keep a 1,000 pound horse in good shape. He'll also eat about 15 pounds of hay in a day and a night. Later, two feedings a day are plenty.

I don't like to put out too much feed to where a horse will

waste it, either. In the summertime, if you put out too much feed, he'll slobber on it. That draws flies and if he should eat more of what he left, later on, he could get worms or some kind of disease. So be sure to put out just what he usually eats, and if he leaves any feed clean it out of his trough before you feed him again.

Where grain's concerned, I've had a whole lot better luck feeding a horse the same amount every day—not a whole lot today and a little tomorrow. Keep his feeding times regular too. He'll eat less in the long run and he'll feel better and do better. Let the horse have water anytime he wants it, of course.

I think oats and bran is about the best horse feed you can use. He won't burn out on that like he may some other feed. Give him about a pound of wheat bran with a gallon of oats. That bran is kind of a laxative and a horse that's kept in a stall a lot will need it. He won't need much bran if he's out to pasture getting green stuff. And if you've got him on a pasture of oats, he'll need almost no bran.

In the winter or early spring you can give the horse two or three tablespoons of cottonseed meal twice a day, in his feed, for about two or three weeks. That'll make him shed some hair like he's supposed to. As for salt and minerals, have that out where he can get to it anytime he wants to.

About once a month I like to take a gallon of bran and pour hot water over it, let the water cool and give this to the horse at night feeding. The day you do this, skip his noon feeding.

This is a tonic. It makes his hair look good and acts as a laxative too. It keeps the horse feeling good and helps his appetite.

Saddling

It won't hurt a bit to work around your horse for a little while before you're ready to put the saddle on him. Doesn't have to be long. Maybe just a few minutes. But it helps you both get better acquainted and he gets so he's used to how you do things.

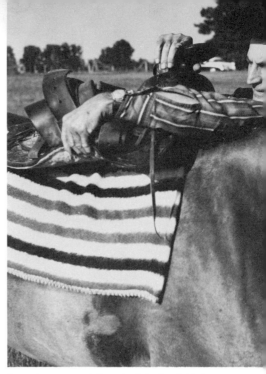

"Make sure you have enough
blanket . . ."

". . . have your girth and girth ring folded
back up on your saddle . . ."

Before you saddle him you can curry him all over with a
rubber brush. It'll take the dirt and loose hair off him. His back
should be cleaned off good.

Make sure you have enough blanket too. It ought to be at
least two inches thick. I like a Navajo blanket myself.

Be sure to check underneath the blanket as you put it on the
horse—to see that there's no hair rolled up under it. The blanket
moving on the horse's back while you're riding can make a little
knot. It's uncomfortable to the horse and can even cause a sore.
It'd be like you having a pebble in your shoe.

Another thing to watch—have your girth and girth ring folded
back up on your saddle when you put the saddle on. That way,
when you swing the saddle up on the horse, the ring won't go
over him and hit his right foreleg. If you hit him many times
with that iron girth ring he'll get pretty nervous when you go to
saddle him.

Be sure the saddle is well up on his withers too. As you tighten

48

the front girth, nudge the horse's left foreleg about a foot forward with your left foot. This keeps his hide from wrinkling under the girth when you pull it up snug.

The Warmup

Remember when you get ready to do anything on your horse that it may take him a while to get used to the idea. In the mornings when you first saddle him up, he can be a little stiff and cold. If it's a young horse, he may want to play some too. If he's got lots of vim he may want to buck a little, but hold him pretty tight for a few minutes and he'll be okay.

That's why you ought to give your horse a good warm up after you put a saddle on him. Walk him around, in circles or just back and forth. Then mount the horse and let him trot in circles and walk for a little while before you start to do much work.

Let him go from a trot to a lope. And if he's feeling frisky, go

"As you tighten the front girth . . ."

". . . nudge the horse's left foreleg . . ."

ahead and let him work up a sweat before you try to do any-thing on him. Get him a little leg weary, then let him rest five or ten minutes before you start whatever it is you want to do on that horse.

He'll do a lot better job of it. Instead of having all that fool-ishness in his head, he'll think he better get down to business.

Riding Habits

While you're making up your mind about how good a horse you've bought, that horse is apt to be making up his mind about how good a rider you are. A pony that's been broke by a horse-man can tell the feel of that horseman. If the man you bought the horse from rode well, the horse will expect you to do the same—at the start. If you don't he'll pretty soon start doing like you do.

It's true that a horse will get to be a lot like the man who rides him. If you ride him sloppy, he'll travel sloppy. If you don't keep yourself collected and gathered-up—your muscles like they should be—then he won't either.

If you get out there and let him walk down the road with you slouched over on one side of the saddle and not sitting up straight, he'll first try to walk under you. That bothers him. Pretty soon he won't care.

Just remember this: The fewer bad habits *you* have, the bet-ter riding horse you're going to have.

That's why you want to give your horse plenty of exercise. It'll help you too. In fact, unless you're roping or cutting on a pony, or using him for ranch work, it's pretty hard to give a horse too much exercise. Most pleasure horses don't get enough.

To keep him hard and in good shape, it'd be good to exercise him every day. Either ride him or lead him at least one hour.

You probably won't want to lope him more than 10 minutes of that time. And I sure wouldn't advise a man to lope a horse on hard gravel or pavement. It's awful rough on a horse's legs and feet.

If your horse is in good shape, it's all right to let him go in a full run once in awhile, for short distances. Taper off your riding by letting the horse trot a ways. Take him on past where you really want to stop, get off and lead him back to where you mean to unsaddle him. This will keep him from getting any set habits on where and when to quit work.

Here's another tip to remember after a ride too: Don't feed your horse or water him while he's still hot. Wait until the sweat begins to dry before you let him have any water. Of course, in the summer if you leave him out in the sun he'll keep on sweating. Most times, you should wait 10 or 15 minutes before letting him get any water.

Bad Habits

Horses can get bad habits the same as people. You can help them get rid of most of these by being just a little smarter than the horse. If you don't think you're as smart as a horse you're not giving yourself enough credit, most likely.

Anyway, I guess one of the worst habits a horse can get into is getting upset every time you want to catch him and saddle him.

Best way to get him over this is to catch him as often as you can when you *don't* want to saddle him. If you've got a few minutes, go out and and give him a handful of feed, talk to him a little—using his name—and pat him some. Just fool with him like you were going to use him. But don't. Next time you do want to use him, he won't run off.

You may find your horse is a little barn-crazy—especially if somebody's been riding him who liked to run him hard just before they stopped riding. Let's say you ride a pony for all he's worth up to your barn or wherever you keep the horse. After a little of that, the horse will get to the certain spot where he started running for home before and he'll want to do it again. He thinks the quicker he gets there the quicker you're going to turn him loose.

If he does this, you can just turn around and go the other way. Then you can approach the barn or stall by another route. If he still keeps trying to break and run toward the barn, turn him around and around. Get him dizzy from this and he'll decide that's not the thing to do. He'll be glad to walk home.

This turning the horse is a lot better punishment than whipping or spurring him. It's one thing a horse can't figure out.

If he's set on running, you can't keep him from it, if he doesn't want you to. If you were on the ground, you might hold him. On his back, you can't.

But you can spin him or run him in a circle until he's tired. Just catch one rein and make him keep turning. Then turn him the other way, if he needs it. Or like the cowboy said: "Unwind him now."

After five minutes of this, he won't care *which* direction he goes.

I don't want to give anybody the idea that you shouldn't slap or switch a horse at all. Sometimes they need it. You shouldn't think so much of a horse that you can't hit him, in the right way, if you need to do that to correct him.

Now say your horse has the habit of wandering to the right or left as you're riding along. For some reason, some horses will do that—they'll just bear off one way or the other. If you let them go, they'll wind up going in a big circle.

If he has the habit of heading over to the left, rein him to the right. If he keeps pulling to the left, slap him on the shoulder with your left foot and spur him behind the girth on the right side. He'll wake up and start watching you and get that left-handedness off his mind.

So it'll pay you to talk to the man you get your horse from about any habits the horse has. Also find out who rode the horse before and what kind of riders they were.

Grooming

In the summer, after you've ridden him, it's good to give your

"In hotter climates you'd want to do this every day or so."

horse a bath. In hotter climates you'd want to do this every day or so. But you wouldn't want to bathe him right after you finish riding the horse. Give him time to cool off.

The way I like to bathe a horse is to use a hose with the nozzle set on fine spray. It's all right to use soap maybe once or twice a week, but not any more often. It'll take too much of the oil out of your horse's hair.

Be sure to wash all the parts where the girths and saddle have been on him. A breast harness can blister him if he isn't used to it, especially when it's hot. (The hair can be rubbed right off.)

After washing, take a paddle and rake the water off the horse. This paddle can be just a flat piece of wood or metal maybe a foot long. You can buy one at most places that sell harness gear and saddles.

Make sure you get him clean, that's the main thing. You won't have a sore-backed horse, sore where the girths go, anyway, if you keep him clean.

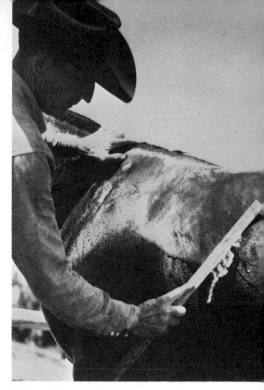

". . . use soap maybe once or twice
a week."

"This paddle can be a flat piece of wood
or metal . . ."

Let him dry naturally. In summer it'll take about 20 minutes
or so. Then you can brush him with a clean brush. If you want
his hair to really look good, go over him with a cotton rag. Rub
him with it the way his hair lays.

You don't have to put any oil on him, but if you want some
extra sheen to his coat, you can use some hair oil. Just like
people use.

Put a little of it—not much, though—on a rag. Rub him all
over with it and it'll make him look glossy. Lot of people do this
who plan to show their horses. If you put too much oil on him,
though, and he gets in any dust, he'll be dirty in 30 minutes.
Most times you can keep your horse looking fine by just a rub-
down with that cotton rag.

Living Quarters

If you have a good horse, you'll find that anybody who comes to see you will want to see him. It's only natural. And you'll want them to. But too many strangers coming around where you keep your horse can sure get on his nerves.

In the first place, if you keep your horse in a stall all the time he's apt to get ill-tempered. Then if strangers keep coming up to him and if they pick at him much, it may cause him to start trying to bite.

If you want to keep people from annoying the horse, just tie him back in the stall, to where his head will be turned away from the door. Don't let him stick his head out of the stall door at all.

The best thing is to give your horse as much room to move around in as you can. It doesn't have to be any big pasture—a patch of ground smaller than a city lot can be plenty for him to exercise himself in. In the winter, naturally, he needs shelter.

"Rub him with it the way his hair lays."

Owning The Quarter Horse

Child Safety With Horses

Some people have the idea that a horse may be risky for small children to play around with. I don't find that to be so. Just the opposite. Most any good-natured horse that's fully grown will take better care of kids than some people.

This is especially so with horses that are old enough to quit using in any kind of contest. They're calm and don't get excited about much of anything. I've seen kids do things with some horses that grown men couldn't do.

For one thing, a horse won't ever walk on a child on purpose. For another, you can put a kid on a horse's back and the horse will just naturally want to be careful. If you were to get on the same horse, he might want to lope off some place. But a horse just seems to know when he has a child on him.

In fact, you put a little kid on your horse, put them in a pen together and the first thing you know that horse will be doing like the kid. He'll have kid ways. The youngster might drop off his back and catch him by the tail. He may ride under a tree and catch hold of a limb.

If you or I did that sort of thing, it might scare the horse. But after a kid has flopped all over a horse's back for a little while, the horse won't be much surprised at anything.

I had one pretty big Quarter Horse awhile back—weighed 1,320 and was about 15 hands high—and my youngest daughter Jan had to climb up him with a rope. She'd shinny up until she got one foot in the stirrup.

She never did make that horse go any faster than a slow lope. She'd lean up over his neck and try to make him go—but do you think he'd hurry? Not hardly. He'd keep going the same speed. Yet that horse was four years old and you let a man get on him, and he'd really move out.

Now I don't mean you can go rope any unbroke horse out of a pasture and put a child on it. Naturally, the horse should be halter broke and good-natured. That's what nearly any good Quarter Horse you get is going to be.

Years ago I began letting my kids get on some horses nobody else had ridden. I'd lead the horse while one of the kids would climb around on his back, getting on and off. Not one horse ever put up a fuss.

In fact, I had one little sorrel filly that was spooky as she could be. But by the time Jan had been sitting on her awhile, swinging bridle reins around, kicking and singing up a storm—well, the horse got so lazy I could hardly get her to go to work.

You can almost bet on it. A bunch of kids can get a horse gentle almost before you can get a saddle on him.

6 TRAINING THE COLT

Training young horses is like training young children. Be firm, be patient and start early.

You can get almost as fond of a colt as you can of a child. You'll want to pet the pony a lot. But don't wait too long before you get a halter on the colt. The longer you wait the more spoiled and hard to handle he can get.

Catch the youngster anywhere from one to two weeks of age and slip on a soft little halter of cotton rope or leather that won't skin him up.

To do this, you need to get the colt in a close place—maybe in one corner of a corral—where he can't run off. You can tie his mother close by so he (and she) won't be too upset.

Ease the colt up close to the fence with your body. Keep your knee and leg up under his belly so he can't kick. Put one arm around his neck and put the halter on him with the other. It'll take a few minutes but he'll stand still after he sees you don't mean to hurt him.

He may rear up and fall over in fighting the rope after he's haltered—but he won't do it long. You can break him to halter in less than half an hour.

One reason I like to get him used to a halter and rope so young is to keep the colt from getting himself hurt later on. As he gets older and stronger, he'll resist the rope more. When he's still a baby, you can keep him from falling on his head, for instance. There's been a lot of horses hurt that way.

Next thing you need to get that colt to do is to follow you at the end of the rope. One good way is to have somebody lead his mama off. He'll naturally want to follow, so you can walk away with the mare and the colt will be leading without knowing it.

Then after half a day or so of that, drop a loop over the colt's rump, run the lead rope through his halter and you can lead him away from the mare. But don't pull on him hard and don't look at him as you lead him.

Lots of horses won't lead if you look at them. In fact, you won't find one horse in 20 that will lead if you walk up and stare at him while you pull on his lead rope. Just turn around and walk off with the colt. He'll follow you if you don't watch him.

In a week or so you'll have him used to it if you work with him maybe five or ten minutes a day.

Another thing he should get used to right away is the feel of a person's hands on him. Rub him all over—down his flanks, under his belly, between his forelegs and hindlegs. This helps to gentle him and may keep him from kicking somebody later on. Most horses kick out to the rear because they're startled or afraid of what's going on behind them. After he knows what hands feel like, he won't be apt to kick when he's in a stall and somebody touches his rump.

Next, get him to where you can pick up his feet. When the colt is young this is easy since you can hold him still. Pick up a foot like you were going to shoe him. Then pat or hit the bottom of that foot with the palm of your hand. Soon he'll know you're not trying to hurt him. He gets used to the feel and noise of it, and he won't get excited later on when he's shod.

After he's used to the halter and the rope and a few people, unless you're going to keep him for a show horse only, I don't think it's good to handle a colt much. Let him learn life by himself. Turn him out to pasture for a year or so and let him find out how to get over logs and rocks and ditches with his mother. If you help him do everything, he'll get so he depends on you for everything.

Of course, a colt will probably need some looking after. And that halter training and gentling will come in handy if he gets scratched up in some barbed wire.

He probably won't jump and fall and fight that rope when you go out to doctor his cuts if he's halter broke when he's little.

Weaning

Seven or eight months is a good time to wean the colt. He'll eat with his mother up to then. And he needs all the green grass he can get while he's on her milk. You can start him on feed before that, of course. As young as three weeks, he'll take oats and bran with his mother. But the grass will give him vitamins he needs too.

I think it's a good idea when you wean the colt, to lead him some and teach him what it's like to be tied to something. I like a swinging limb just above the colt's head and away from any fence—so that if he jumps back he won't stick a foot in it.

You can leave him tied to that limb for, say, two hours at a time, in the morning and again in the afternoon. As you lead him back and forth from his stall or corral, he'll also get better acquainted with you. If you're planning to show him at halter later on, this is a good time to start teaching him how to stand— while he's tied to that limb. He can get to know what you mean by standing on all four feet.

61

As for his feed, you can take him right off his mother at eight months and put him on bran, oats or some kind of sweet feed and he'll do all right on it. You'll have to suit this to the climate and part of the country you're in.

And this is a good time to teach the colt to load in a trailer. Just push your trailer up to a fence and tie it there. If it's a two-wheel trailer, jack up the hitch end and feed him inside it. Don't feed him anywhere else for a week or two and he'll get so he won't mind getting in.

If you have a two-horse trailer and two colts, put them both in it for feeding. Then they'll get used to rocking it back and forth as they move around. In fact, I've seen a few trailer bodies, with no wheels on them, swung inside a stall from overhead rods. The horses go in and get used to the motion and learn how to balance themselves.

Naturally, a horse will be suspicious of a trailer if he hasn't been in one before. Simplest way to get him to go in there is with feed in a pan or bucket. Show him he has to follow you in the trailer to get at that feed. If he's hungry, he'll get in.

After weaning, the colt needs another six to eight months to grow before you start any more training. Of course, you can take him to a halter show anytime now.

Fifteen months is a good time to start getting him used to other kinds of rope. First, he ought to learn about hobbling and sidelining.

Hobbling And Sidelining

A hobble is a piece of rope around his front or back feet to make the horse stand still. A sideline rope is the same only it runs from a front foot to a back one. Teaching the horse to get used to these ropes teaches him to stay calm when he gets his feet tangled up later on in a piece of rope or wire.

He'll learn to stand still until you come and free him. He'll learn that it doesn't do any good to fight the rope. He'll also

 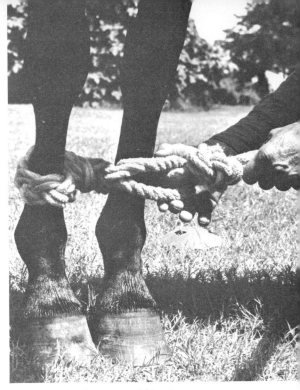

"... put one twist in it between his legs." "Tie it in the loop around the leg nearest you."

learn to depend a little on you too. He soon finds out that when he stands still, you take the rope off.

Be sure not to use anything as rough as grass ropes for your hobbles—that would be apt to "burn" his hide. Soft one-inch cotton rope is better. What I like to do is undo the rope and plait the three strands into a flat strip, about two inches wide. You want an eye or loop in the end of it.

To hobble his front legs, throw the end of this plaited rope around the leg on the opposite side from you. Then put one twist in it between his legs. Tie it in the loop around the leg nearest you.

Then let the rope drop down so it's between the colt's feet and ankles. It shouldn't be so tight that it pulls his feet together, but tight enough to keep him from moving more than a foot or so at a time.

Next, hobble him on the back feet. This makes it almost impossible for the horse to do much moving around.

Training The Colt

Finally, get your horse used to sidelines and cross-sidelines. To side line a horse means to hook his front and hind foot, on the same side, together. Be sure not to turn him loose this way, though. He can still cover a lot of acres like that. Cross-sidelining is more awkward. This is roping a front foot to the opposite back foot. He won't fight this as long because he can't do anything about it.

I like to cross-sideline a colt once a day for about a week. It's one of the best things you can do to make sure a horse won't run off if his reins are dropped on the ground.

About half an hour at a stretch is long enough to leave a horse hobbled or sidelined.

Hackamore Training

When the pony is between 14 and 16 months old you can start driving him ahead of you with a hackamore halter and reins. I don't think it hurts to put a saddle on him to do this. He gets

". . . get your horse used to sidelines . . ."

"About half an hour at a stretch is long enough."

used to the saddle and also you can run the lines from the hacka-more back through the stirrups. Be sure to tie the stirrups to-gether under his belly. We talked about saddling a horse in the last chapter so I won't go back over it again here.

With the saddle on him, be sure you have at least eight or ten feet of line coming out behind him from his hackamore. It's a good idea too for you to start this part of his training in a corral or arena so that if he gets excited he can't go far.

When you first start to drive a pony, have somebody lead him for awhile with you coming along behind. Then after five or ten minutes that person can turn him loose and you can go ahead and drive him pretty well. He understands by then what's go-ing on.

First thing you want to do is teach him to stop. And every time you say "Whoa" be sure to use his name. It won't be long before he'll know you mean him when you say his name.

When you stop him, be quiet and gentle and don't scare him. You want to drive him with his head straight, lined up with the saddle horn in front of you, and you want him to stop the same way.

Pull on both of your lines the same. He should stop with his head straight, not up in the air.

Next try him in a turn to the right. Pull on the right line but hold a little tension on the left one. This should help him turn with his body straight. You don't want a limber-necked horse that turns his head way over to the side.

Same thing in a left turn. Pull your left line with the right one just tight enough to keep his head and body straight.

When you have him turning and stopping, tell him to "back." He probably won't want to, but there's not much he can do about it.

You can pull back, gentle but firm, on both lines hard enough so that he'll have to back up. If he's a pretty good Quarter Horse, he'll weigh somewhere around 800 pounds at this point.

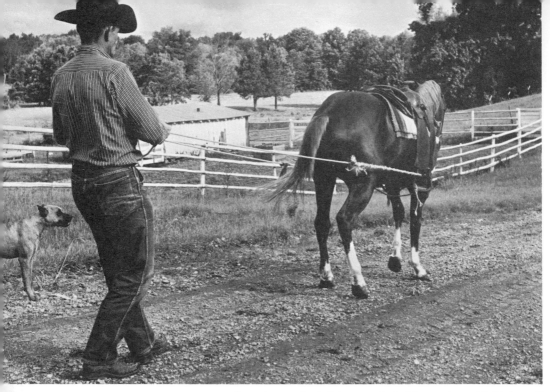

". . . have at least eight or ten feet of line coming out behind . . ."

If you were on his back, you couldn't hold him. On the ground behind him, if he's not too excited, you can.

Here's another thing—give him your voice command first, then wait a second before you either stop him or back him. Later on, he should start doing what you want when he hears your voice.

This training with long lines should go on about 15 to 20 days, but not every day. Drive him for four or five days, then skip one or two. The first day or so you work him like this, just do it for ten minutes or so. Later you can work him 30 minutes at a time. But don't work him until you see that he's aggravated or tired out.

In a week or so you'll have him used to the work enough so that you can drive him in a short gallop. You'll have to trot along behind—and this can get to be work. But if you keep at this, you'll have a horse that will respond to the least touch on that hackamore and won't be foolish about throwing his head around.

After each time you work him, be sure to drive him away from your barn or shed or wherever you're going to take the equipment off him. Stop him straight, going away from the barn, and he won't get so he wants to run to it whenever he gets a notion it's almost time to quit work. Also, pet him for a little while and talk to him, to let him get the idea that he did what you wanted him to. Then lead him back to the barn by the hackamore reins.

The Snaffle Bit

While you're driving him with the hackamore, you can also get him used to the snaffle bit.

But you don't want to give him too much of it all at once. If you put it on him and turned him out to pasture, it would make

". . . help him turn with his body straight."

67

his mouth sore—it would be about like you holding a spoon in your mouth cross-ways.

So put it on him after you've been driving him awhile with the hackamore, but don't put any reins to the bit yet. Just put on a bridle with the snaffle but go ahead handling and driving the pony with the hackamore.

After he gets to where he doesn't chew the bit, and the corners of his mouth start to toughen, he's getting used to it.

Now let him wear the bit two weeks, and it doesn't matter if he wears it all day. Let him eat and drink with it on.

Then you can take the hackamore off, put the long reins onto the bridle and drive him with that snaffle bit. Be sure when you stop him that you don't pull so hard that he starts slinging his head. Be gentle and when you say "Whoa" he'll stop just like he did with the hackamore on him.

Starting To Ride The Pony

By the time he's 18 to 20 months old, the horse is old enough to ride. When you first go to ride him, put the hackamore back on. And you won't break many horses before you'll find that they all don't wear it best in the same place. Some are sensitive on their nose in one place, some another.

Put the hackamore on him too low and he may feel he's being sort of smothered. He'll throw his head down to fight it. Put it on him too high and he'll sling his head up. You'll have to adjust it up or down until you find where each pony likes it best.

Another thing. Lots of horses will have a hard mouth, and you'll be able to hold them with a hackamore where you couldn't hold them with a bit. Those that have a soft mouth are held easy with almost anything. You won't find too many iron-jawed horses among good Quarter Horses. Soft mouths are bred in them nowadays just like speed and conformation.

But some people make this mistake with their horses—they try to ride the animal with something that doesn't fit and which the horse doesn't like. You want to use just as light a bit as you can use to handle him, without hurting him. You want enough "port" in it (where his tongue goes) so that when you pull on your reins, there's a place for his tongue without catching it between jawbone and the bit.

A spade bit is all right if you know how to use it. It has a copper roller to keep the horse's mouth moist and full of saliva. The horse with a soft mouth isn't apt to get hurt. If it's dry, though, you can sure pinch a horse's mouth with a spade bit. I think there's been more good horses ruined by people riding them with pretty bits instead of bits that fit.

Now let's say you're ready for your first ride. You shouldn't have to tie him to get on. But you should catch your left rein shorter than the right, and hold them both in your left hand up along side of his neck. Then if anything scares him as you mount, he'll jump with his heels away from you. In other words, the short left rein will turn him into a spin.

But if you've gone through the gentling and training I've outlined, you shouldn't have any trouble getting on the horse. Sit there a couple of minutes and get off.

It won't be but a few days before you can get on and off him from either side.

If when you first get on the pony he feels like he's going to buck—well, you've got your left rein tighter as you get on, so just keep him that way so he'll move in a circle if he moves. But don't let him break away and run.

That's why it's a good idea to be in a round corral or arena, not over 30 feet or so across. Keep him in there for the first few days you ride him. You don't want him to buck, so don't get off if he gets excited and starts acting up. Keep him in a circle and he'll quiet down. Ride him maybe 15 or 20 minutes at a time after the first few days of getting on and off, then start adding five minutes a day to the time you ride him until you're riding about an hour a day. That's enough riding each day for the first 30 days you ride him.

Training The Colt

Teaching The Pony His ABC's

The young horse is about 18 months old by the time he gets used to being ridden and has a rough idea of what it's like to have somebody on his back, wanting him to do first one thing and then another.

It's time now to show him some of the things he'll have to know, no matter what use you're going to make of him.

First, he'll have to be ridden in a straight trot. Get him in a bigger arena or down a dirt road someplace. In a straight trot, he learns how to work every leg the same, to carry his feet and set them where they should be.

And here's something you don't want to forget: When you ride this pony away from your house or barn, take a hobble along.

After you've been run off from a few times you'll get so you'll remember to keep a hobble with you when you go off on a horse that's only partly trained. Walking a few miles across a rocky pasture can sure help your memory. So take the hobble with you, hung on the saddle horn, and when you get off for any reason just tie it around the pony's ankles.

He can learn to move away with hobbles on his front feet but he won't get out of sight. Hobbled on his back legs, he won't move much at all.

After the trot, let him move into a lope for awhile. Right in here you can start teaching him to move into left and right leads. He'll need to know this if you ever enter any Quarter Horse reining contests, and it also helps him get so he'll take new orders in a hurry. Here's how:

When you go into a slow lope, move the pony to the left, say, and shift your weight to the left. As you move in a big left hand circle he will get under your weight and lead with his left foreleg.

After that, stop him and do the same thing in a right hand circle. Then you're ready, after some more practice, to lope through some left hand circles, and without stopping, change into a right hand circle. This figure eight will make the horse change leads, as he goes from one to the other. Make those circles round, though, and not always the same size—you don't want your pony figuring that all figure eights have the same size or number of turns. He wouldn't rein right if he kept in the same pattern.

Now you want to lope the horse straight and stop him the same way. When he stops, pull him back a few steps and make him stand there for four or five seconds. This is to calm him.

As you move him away from that spot, don't go forward. Let him move back another step or two and turn him as he backs. There's two reasons for this. If you go forward after you've stopped him, he'll get so his stops won't be sharp and clean—he'll be expecting to just go on forward next, anyhow. So you want to always pivot him after a stop.

Then if you turn him as he backs, he'll get so he'll pivot on his hind feet the way he should, with his head and body all in line.

To back the horse—something else he has to know now—you'll need to shift your weight to the rear of the saddle at the same time you put a little pull on the reins. But again, don't pull too much. Give him the word "back," then the weight shift and reining. He should keep his head down as he backs.

After the horse learns these things, he needs something else more than training. He needs some time to grow. That's why I'd turn him out to pasture when he's 18 to 20 months and you've broke him to the saddle.

Of course, you can show him at halter competitions while he's this age, but I wouldn't advise a man who didn't have lots of experience with colts to do any roping or hard work on a horse this young. Give him six months just to grow. He'll do a lot of growing in six months.

Breaking The Older Colt

There may be times when you'll want to train an older colt

you've bought from somebody who didn't halter break the horse at all. One of the first things I'd do with a young horse like this is to make friends with the horse, with feed, like I outlined in the last chapter. This is a good idea for any horse you get that hasn't been well-broke.

After that you'll want to get the horse used to a hackamore. First, get a rope around his neck and work him into a stall. Get his hindquarters into one corner so that his head is toward you. It'll take some time but finally you can get a hackamore on him.

Be sure it fits and is strong enough so he won't break it. Then tie a one-inch rope about 15 feet long to the hackamore. You can turn him into a big corral and let him wear this for three or four days. He will step on that rope and learn to respect it quite a bit.

Next, catch him and start leading him in the corral. You do this by walking around him. The rope will make him turn as you go. Just make your circles a little larger each time and you'll soon be leading him.

Then tie him to a solid wall(not a fence where he can stick his foot through a crack) half a day at a time for four or five days. He sure to tie him to something higher than his withers. Be around him during this time. Brush him and lay an old saddle blanket on him now and then.

Do as much around him as you can—but do it quietly and let him know that you're not going to hurt him. After that he's ready for saddling.

Deciding His Future

Up to the time a horse is two years old he's sort of like a child. He'll get his own exercise. Where there's more than one, young horses will run and play like kids. But the two year old pony, even if he's a well-broke horse, still doesn't have all his growth, and most of them don't know how to run and carry weight. It's time now for him to learn that and some other things too.

Best thing here is to get him in a large arena or on some good pasture land, without any rocks around, where the dirt is loose. If you try to run him and work him in more than a couple of inches of dirt, or in loose sand, he'll have a hard time running. An ordinary roping arena—about 40 yards wide and 100 yards long—is fine.

You're not trying to see how fast he can go yet, or how far. You want to train him to get started in a hurry and be able to stop or turn the same way.

And since running hard is still new to him, you have to help a little. You can use a switch on him—something like a small strip of leather, or maybe the end of a bridle rein. Anything will do that makes a popping noise. He'll get the idea right away what you want him to do.

Some horsemen let a young pony run with an older horse for a little while. Chasing calves for short distances also helps him get up speed. But you should keep these early runs under 100 yards.

You should practice making him run from a standing start, mostly. Run him for about 50 yards or so then stop him. When you do, be sure to shift your weight back as you call out "Whoa" —do it just a second before you pick up on the reins. That way he knows what's coming by your weight shift.

Pick up on your reins straight—so he'll stop that way. And don't try to grind him right down into the ground the first few times. He has to get the feel of stopping, like everything else.

It'll take your pony several days of work to run wide open and come to a sliding stop. Start running him shorter distances and stopping, too. Pretty soon, he'll go wide open from a standing start and be able to stop within 20 feet.

You can run him and stop in less distance than that with practice, but now you might try him down a fence line. You can get an idea from this what kind of "action" he's apt to have.

Run him down the fence, stop him and turn him into the fence at the same time. To keep his head from hitting the fence, he'll have to slide, squat and roll back over his hocks.

" . . . he'll go wide open . . . and stop within 20 feet."

Work him that way in both directions, down both fence lines. After you do, you'll start to get an idea of what kind of horse you've got. But there's something else you need to know about your Quarter Horse—does he have any cow sense?

To find out, you can do some work on him around cattle. I don't mean work him all day—an hour or so a day is enough for now.

When you get him around cattle you want to watch and see if he's interested in those cattle. If he looks at them and watches what they do, that's a good sign.

If you run him over to head off a cow and he's willing to do it, he shows signs of working with his head. But don't overdo cow-work on him yet. If he's only two years old or so and still learning to run and break away fast, he'll let some cows get away from him. First thing you know, he'll be letting them all get away.

That's why you can't push the pony. Mostly, you want to work cattle or other livestock pretty easy on him, practice starting and stopping and see what things he can do best.

If he hasn't forgotten what you taught him before, you have a smart horse. If he's willing to work, it means he's not lazy— you do find some horses that are. The lazy kind take more training to do anything.

If your horse has lots of early speed, you can feel pretty sure you have the makings of a roping horse. For that, he needs to be able to break and run good for 150 yards—then be able to stop no matter how fast he's going. You want him to run up on a calf and have the cow sense to slow to the same speed as the calf.

If your horse is extra calm and yet can pivot good and roll back over his hocks easy, you may have a cutting horse.

If his conformation is good and he has a soft mouth and reins like you want him to, you have a winner for halter shows or reining contests.

And if the horse has strength, if he's calm and has cow sense, you've sure got a good ranch horse to work on.

75

But you don't have to make up your mind what you're going to make out of him yet. In fact, it's a good idea to turn a two year old pony out for a two week rest period every few months. Don't ride him at all during those rests.

The horse still has some growing to do.

7 TRAINING THE CUTTING HORSE

The cutting horse has sure come a long way from the time when the first cowboy pushed his pony into a herd and cut out the cattle he wanted to sell or doctor.

In those early days, you used the same horses for everything. You'd ride out to fix fences, chase wolves, round up cattle, go to town—just about anything you needed to do on a horse, your horse would have to be able to do it.

Then the big cowmen found out that some cow ponies could head a cow faster and easier than others. The horses that had the best action and the most cow sense were saved, after that, until the boss got his herd to where he wanted it split up.

This was back before they had pens and chutes to divide a herd. Then, the horse and rider had the job of moving into a herd, picking out the cattle to be cut out, and easing them over to a spot away from the main herd.

The Cutting Horse

It took some doing in those days. Those old Longhorn cattle knew what to do with those horns, so the cutting horses had it rough sometime, and the cowboys to. They had to take each cow or steer from the main herd without getting the other cattle riled up, and had to drive each animal maybe 100-200 yards away—with the critter trying to get back to the herd every little ways.

The idea was to never let a cow stop. You had to keep her moving toward the "cut"—those animals you were cutting out of the herd.

Which meant the cutting horse had to move in an instant, stop quick and be one thought ahead of those cattle. I've seen a cutting horse down in some awful positions—almost down on the ground, spread out like an ink blotter. But it wouldn't make any difference which way the cow went—she was looking right square in that horse's eye when she stopped.

Ranch cutting now hasn't changed much—except there isn't as much of it done on horseback. In lots of cases, herds can be split up faster and easier with pens and chutes. But cutting is getting more popular all the time as a sport. The cutting horse is nearly always a registered Quarter Horse nowadays, and he's been taugh his trade so well that lots of old time cowboys wouldn't believe it unless they could see a modern cutting contest.

As a sport, cutting started as just an exibition event in some of the big rodeos. Then after the Quarter Horse became a breed in 1940, and rules for cutting contests were set up, the National Cutting Horse Association was organized. That was in 1946. Now it has lots of affiliates going all over the country—in more than 40 states at the last count. Something over 7,000 people in this country, Canada, Mexico and Arabia compete with cutting horses, the NCHA people figure.

So even though only the biggest ranches still do much range cutting, you can see this kind of horse perform just about any place where there's a horse show or rodeo.

The reason so many people like the sport is that almost anybody who can ride pretty good can have fun—and maybe even win something—with a cutting horse. A big part of the cutting horse owners now aren't cowboys by trade. They're doctors, grocers, drug store owners, high school kids—everyday people who can afford a pretty good horse and have the time to work with him some.

And it does take work to get any cutting horse into shape for a contest. Lots of the cutting horse clubs have weekly or monthly contests to warm up for shows. And the people who win most are those who spend the most time working on their horse and themselves.

Once you get through reading this chapter I hope you'll have tips that'll help you get good results with your cutting horse—but don't think it's just a matter of that *horse* learning. You want to ride better than average if you expect to do a lot of contesting, and *you* sure have to have some "cow sense" just like your horse.

We're going to talk mostly here about training a Quarter Horse for contest cutting. Those contests are why the animal is now so well-bred and valuable. But a cutting horse, no matter how pretty, just isn't, unless he has the same kind of range savvy that helped his ancestors do their work 90 years ago.

Cow Sense

Up until he's about three years old and well broke, it's hard to tell for sure if a horse is going to make a good cutting horse. He doesn't get all his growth until about seven years, and it's risky to do much hard work on him before he's three or four years old.

But you can tell whether a horse has much cow sense before he's three. Lots of cowmen swear that horses either are born with it or else they don't have it.

To find out how your horse will act around cattle, take him to some. Ride him into a pasture—or big arena will do—and let him watch a few cows from a little distance. If he'll look at those cows pretty steady and take an interest in them, you have a good chance of him making a cutting horse.

Pick out a cow a little distance from the rest of the cattle and walk your horse toward her, slow. Try to pick a slow-motioned old cow that won't do much. When she stops, you stop. Work around so she has to get by you to reach the main herd. When the cow moves, ease your horse over in front of her just fast enough to stop her. This shows how quick your horse will get the idea that you want to keep the cow out of the herd.

I like to ride a horse behind a small bunch of cattle that are moving along. If he has cow sense, the horse will get to watching them. He may even want to nip at them or he might back his ears at them.

If a cow stops, he'll get so he'll stop. He'll want this cow to go on. With the least touch on your reins, he'll move over to make this cow go on into the herd. You won't have to help him much. If a cow walks or trots from the herd, you'll find the horse wants to go see about that.

If he doesn't really have cow sense, and is what I call 'not interested,' you have to rein him or spur him every time to make him go around a cow. It'd take too much time and hard labor to make a cutting horse out of one like this, and then he still might be one you couldn't win on. He just wouldn't be ambitious enough. And he's got to have ambition.

I don't mean you ought to give up the minute it looks like your horse is looking someplace besides at those cattle. You find some young horses that are just naturally slow to catch on. Others may be a little lazy—but they can grow out of it. Remember that a three year old horse is sort of like a kid in the third grade. His attention will wander like the kid's. He's just learning.

By the time the horse is three and you've had him around cattle for a few months, you can try him in an arena with some calves. Yearlings are best since that's what you'll work with in most good cutting contests. But any size calves will do to start with.

Any except Brahman calves or cows. They're a good breed for beef raising, like everybody knows, but for cutting practice they can be awful unpredictable. Until your horse is pretty far along, I'd rather use Herefords.

And I wouldn't use spoiled cattle either. Cattle that have been used a lot by cutting horses will get smart. They'll even get away from an old trained horse. Spoiled cattle will just stick their heads under your horse's neck and go on by, no matter what. I've seen them push horses away from a fence to get by. They've caught on that they won't get hurt.

You're fixing to ruin your young horse if you keep trying to make him hold cattle back that are impossible to hold. Once a cow makes up her mind to get back to a herd, that's where she'll go, if she has gotten away a few times.

Goats are good practice—for a few days. But they'll start to run under a horse too. They're hard to hold, and a pony learns that he has to watch a goat close. It's a good way for some horses (that don't do it naturally) to learn to work with their heads down. The pony finds he has to jump and bow his head fast to turn that goat.

You have to go easy on this, though. Once the goat starts running under the horse, the horse will get mad and go to biting at the goat. He'll even try to paw it with his feet. He shouldn't be worked on goats too long at one time.

In The Arena

When you start working your pony on cows or calves in an arena, you'll need at least one turn-back man on horseback— or maybe two if it's a wide arena—to keep the animal you're working in position.

Another thing I like to do when I start a horse on arena cutting is to put a rope or wire around his neck for most of the reining. You'd want to carry this rope or wire down where his

"... move your horse into the herd slow ..."

breast harness would be, just above the point of his shoulders. Then ride the horse with the reins in one hand and your rope in the other.

The idea is to "stay off his head." I mean by this—don't put any more pressure on his bit with your reins than you have to. Some riders get to jerking a horse's mouth so much that the horse won't do things real fast. He's afraid he'll get jerked for it.

And you want your cutting horse to move fast when he moves. So give him all the slack on the reins he wants. Then when he jabs to the right or left with his head, the bit won't jerk him.

That's part of the big difference between a ranch and a contest cutting horse. To the ranch horse, a slack rein means for him to quit that particular cow. Just the opposite with a show cutting horse. Give him plenty of slack while he's working, then pick up on the reins when you're through with the cow. Put your hand on his neck for him to stop.

82

We'll say you're going to start on yearling calves. Well then, move your horse into the herd slow and nose one out. Get the calf 40 to 50 feet out from the herd and let your horse stand there and watch it.

If the calf runs up the arena, the turnback men will send it back. Just sit there and don't move your pony until the calf moves to get back to the herd. This is the hardest part of training a cutting horse. Patience. Most people don't have enough. They won't wait.

As long as the calf stands still, you make your horse stand still. Don't move him to make the calf move. You're trying to teach him to hold that calf—to keep it out there away from the herd. You don't want to make it do something—the animal should do that itself. In training, of course, you can nod to a turnback man to ease up and get the calf going it if spends more than a minute in one spot. (If it does, you may have picked a poor calf to work in the first place.)

"You're trying to teach him to hold that calf . . ."

"... go into the fence in position to come away from it smooth and fast."

Anyway, keep your horse facing the calf. When it starts toward the herd you nudge and rein your horse along at the same speed to head the calf. If you see the horse will be late, spur him. But be careful.

I wouldn't advise anybody to spur a young horse much. Makes them spur happy. I think it's a good idea to wear spurs but I don't use them much. Just let the horse know you have them on and what they're for. In most cases, you can squeeze him with your legs and he'll respond.

Now about the calf. If you're working a young horse, you'll have to watch the animal you're cutting as close as your horse does. Pretty soon you'll get the feel of which way the calf's about to go. It will move one ear or cut its eyes one way or another. Of course a real wild cow won't do that much. She doesn't know where she's going anyway. She's just trying to get away, somehow.

When the calf you're working breaks toward the fence, try

84

to make your horse go into the fence in position to come away from it smooth and fast. That's what the calf may do. It may also try to squeeze by your horse if it beats you to the fence. But if you're at the fence with the calf, it won't try to squeeze by unless you're using the kind of over-used, spoiled cattle I mentioned.

I like to start a young horse to working about 20 to 30 feet from the calf. The horse may soon get to where he wants to charge in close. It can be *too close* real quick. The calf just jumps in and the horse can't roll back to get in front of it fast enough. So if he stays back from the calf while it's ducking and dodging, he can have room to move over in time. As the horse gets older, you can work him in closer.

Practice Times

In the first few sessions, I wouldn't work a horse more than two or three minutes each on maybe three or four calves. You could spread this work out over a couple of hours though. You'd want to fool around the arena enough so the horse gets used to it. Maybe you'd watch somebody else cut some calves on another horse for part of the time.

If your horse did good, you'd want to get off, pat the pony enough so he knows it, and use his name a lot. If he didn't do right, don't pet him. But don't abuse him either because he made some mistakes. You'll make some too.

The time you'll spend working your horse will depend a lot on how your horse feels. It won't be long until you can tell if he likes what he's doing.

At first, you want to be careful about overwork. I don't think a man ought to work a horse at cutting more than about three times a week. But the young horse should be ridden enough— or led around—to keep him hard. A pony working a good cow real fast for more than two minutes has to be in shape.

In cutting contest, you'll have two and a half minute periods to show how good your horse can cut cattle. If you spend most of that time maneuvering, the horse will be in quite a strain. Especially if it's in hot weather.

So as the horse gets older and learns more—after six months, say—you'll want to increase his working time. You'd want him hard enough to work for five or six minutes. And you'd want to work different lengths of time.

The reason for that is so he won't get the idea that after he's worked two minutes, he's all through. You work a horse very long for just two minutes and he'll decide that two minutes is enough from then on. If you get him so that he's still got some go left in him after five minutes, you won't have to worry about drawing cattle at some contest that sure enough move, and then find your horse getting all tired out before your time is up.

I've seen some horses that would work fine for about two minutes then throw their heads up and want to quit. If your horse can work for more than five minutes, you've got a pony with ambition and strength. It takes both to make a real good cutting horse.

Quitting Time

After every workout, when you're ready to quit for the day, don't just lope your pony away from the herd. Turn him around to face the cattle. Let him watch them a minute or two. Get off and loosen your cinch and let him rest some. But keep his mind on those cattle. The idea is to keep him from getting anxious to quit. If he loses interest or gets tired, he'll want to get through and go on up the arena to where the turnback horse is.

But you're in no hurry. Keep him facing those cattle and when you do ride him away from them, do it in a walk.

Getting Him Used To The Unexpected

The seasoned cutting horse is consistent. He's not upset by being in different places or seeing things he hasn't seen before.

That's why—after you've been working your pony in an arena for a few weeks—you want to change things around a little.

You can throw a gunny sack over the fence or roll a barrel up into one corner of the arena, just before you cut some calves that day. These are things for him to notice. He'll see them and he'll know they weren't there last time he was there.

Of course you want to put these things where he won't run into them. But it doesn't hurt once in awhile to let another horseman get in your way while you're working your pony. It can be a turnback man or somebody holding a herd. This way you can find out just how interested your horse is in working that calf. He should keep right on working, no matter what.

Every day you might put something around the arena that wasn't there the day before. Hang something on a fence post one day. Tie some horses just outside the fence.

Don't think your horse won't see these things. A young cutting horse can get upset over things maybe you don't even see yourself. I remember working a pony one day that wasn't acting right and couldn't figure why he kept looking off beyond the arena toward a road. Then I saw a woman walking along with a fishing pole on her shoulder. This bothered that horse until she had walked up to the arena and on out of sight down the road. A friend of mine that was there told me the horse just wanted to go fishing.

If you plan to enter cutting contests right away, it doesn't hurt to get your horse used to noise also. Simplest way to do this is just put an old radio in your barn, near his stall, and play it a lot. Doesn't matter what he hears, he can't sing anyway. You just want him to hear some racket. Let it play long enough and he'll hear plenty. Then when he gets to a show, the music and noise won't bother him as much.

Before you took him to a contest though, it'd be a good idea to cut some cattle in somebody else's arena or pen—even if you have to haul him a few miles to do it. If you work him in just one place all the time, he'll get so he'll know just how to head a cow the easiest for that pen. Put your horse in a strange pen—one that's built a little different shape—and he's really got to work and not just wander around.

Competition Tips

Once a cutting horse has been worked and trained for, say, four to six months, he may be ready for some novice competition. I've seen some ponies win that hadn't been ridden but 90 days. But you won't have a finished cutting horse in much less than a year or two. That's why you want to start him in some contests as soon after six month's training as you can.

If you're just starting into cutting competition yourself, you'll have as much to learn yet as that horse. A lot of amateur horsemen make the big mistake right off of spurring their ponies, trying to control every action. They overdo it instead.

Once your cutting horse knows his job, he should be able to work without a bridle—with just a rope around his neck. (You wouldn't do that in a show, of course.) He doesn't need—and sure doesn't want—a lot of pressure from your heels or reins. He needs just a very little help in avoiding mistakes.

One thing you can do to help him is to pick out a calf or cow, everytime you go into a herd, that will make him work hard. You can't do your horse any good by working some slow motion cow in a contest that doesn't show the pony off right.

Also, you need to know how to make your pony squat down and turn. Don't just get him out there and try to hold a cow back by doing a bunch of spread-out figure eights back and forth across the arena. And a judge likes to see a horse with some vim—one that looks like he sees everything in front of him from a grasshopper to a gobbler.

If your cutting horse is one you've trained yourself, and you're bringing him along just right, you'd want to be careful too about novice riders using him. Even an older horse can pick up bad habits quick from an inexperienced rider.

The amateur rider can help himself a lot by determination. I've seen some that were good riders, but too many times they didn't win as much as they could have just because they didn't *try* hard enough to win. That comes out in your horse and the way you train him.

If you go on the road to a few shows and contests, there's some things you need to get prepared for.

You'll find it hard to get a horse to the peak of condition for cutting and keep him there very long while you're traveling.

For one thing, he can get barn sour. People will want to come and look at your horse, no matter where he's stabled. Lights may be on there up to 18 hours a day. It would irritate anybody.

It's a little hard to take a stallion on the road too. He'll have his mind on other things a lot and if you have to spend the night in some little town, it's next to impossible to find a place that'll keep a stud overnight. Pick your stops ahead of time with that in mind.

". . . you need to know how to make your pony squat down and turn."

The Cutting Horse

It's a little easier to travel with mares or geldings.

But with all the problems of travel, it's a big thrill to win your first show with your own horse. You get a lot more than prize money or trophies too. You wind up wanting to learn even more about that horse and how far he can go. Even if you lose, you've enjoyed yourself.

If you don't win as often as you think you should, don't feel bad. Your Quarter Horses can win at other things most likely. Plenty of top Quarter Horses aren't champions at any one thing but win now and then at several.

They're just like people. One boy will wind up a baseball player. His brother may play a fiddle.

8 TRAINING THE ROPING HORSE

On ranches after the Civil War roping was no sport. It was
work. And it was done a little different than you see it at most
shows and rodeos today.

Western ranches didn't have any fences then and cowboys
didn't have pens to work cattle in. (Pens came along in the
90's). The cattle were still on the open range and had to be
worked from horseback.

If a cow had to be roped for branding, one cowboy would
rope her horns, another her hind feet, and they'll pull her down.
Then they'd stretch her out to hold her there. Of course, if a
cowboy was by himself and had to rope a cow, he could still do
it all right.

He'd throw his loop over the cow's neck, then drop the slack
behind her and jerk her down.

This was kind of rough on cattle but it had to be done lots of times on a ranch—and still does sometimes. Maybe a cow will get something in her foot, you'll need to doctor her and it's too far to a corral. She'll have to be roped and thrown.

You still see cow and steer roping at rodeos in Arizona and California where team roping is a big thing. But at most rodeos and at Quarter Horse performance contests, you'll see mostly calf roping. "Tie-down" roping it's called, because you rope the calf then tie three of its legs together.

You might say there's three kinds of calf roping. There's the kind you do on a ranch, where speed usually doesn't count. There's rodeo roping where speed *does* count. Then there's Quarter Horse performance roping—what counts is *how* your horse helps you do the job.

As far as what *you* do as the roper and what you expect your horse to do, there's not much difference in any of these. Mostly it's an event of skill—a man and a horse working together.

But what makes roping interesting for people to watch is not only teamwork, but that third party in the arena—the calf.

Good lively calves can help you or hurt your chances in both a rodeo or performance contest. Some can be too slow and too small.

Others can get too big and too mean. Lots of calves from Texas are used on the rodeo circuit up through the East. By the time they've been roped in St. Jo, New York, and Boston, they're mighty tough. They can almost tie *you* down. They have to be tough to last through that much roping.

Roping As A Sport

It's easy to see how roping got started back in the early days as a rodeo event. Cowboys started to get good with a rope. One rancher would bet a neighbor that his boys could beat the other's and they started holding contests when they finished work.

It wasn't long before the word got around about these contests. People would come from all over to see them, and they caught rodeo fever from that. It was more than just a contest to see who could rope best, too. It was also to see who had the best horses.

The other rodeo events came on about the same way. Good cutting horses got to competing against each other. The bronc riders tried to see who could stay on wild Mustangs the longest. Things like bull riding and bulldogging don't have much real reason for being, except a cowboy was always ready to try and do anything his buddy could do. And maybe something to boot.

Roping As Work

Now, with fences and pens, cowboys on western ranches don't have to do near as much roping as before. You can handle cattle faster and easier with chutes that separate those you want to cut out of a herd for some reason. But a man who works around livestock still has to be able to rope a cow or a steer—and he wouldn't be a very smart cowboy if he didn't teach his horse something about what to do when there's roping to be done. Which is why most working ranches now have good-bred Quarter Horses. You won't find many that don't make good roping ponies. That's one of the things they were bred to do in the first place.

Of course, a working cow pony probably won't get the amount of training for roping that a contest roping horse will. Things aren't the same on a ranch as in some arena. The ranch hand who wants to rope some crippled calf isn't trying to ruin the brakes on a stop watch, and he's going to be a lot more gentle stopping that calf. So he's not so particular about how quick his horse stops or works a rope, just so long as he can down the calf long enough to doctor it.

In fact, you can give a ranch horse too *much* roping training, if you're not careful. I've had them so they were a little slow to work cattle after going to a few rodeos. They'd want to get behind the cow and chase her—like they'd done at the rodeo. This is not so good when you're trying to turn a cow some way.

This is why some big ranches have horses that are specially

trained for roping, just like some have ponies trained for only cutting. All cow ponies soon get used to the rope being used around them, but if there's a lot of roping to be done, the cowboys will switch to the roping horses.

On smaller ranches, naturally, fewer horses have to be able to do more jobs. And roping is one of the first things they learn.

Picking The Good Roping Horse

If I were naming the things I think a good roping pony *has* to have, I'd say good withers first, then strong forequarters and hindquarters.

He's sure got to have good withers. You want them high enough so you can pad him good. That cow or calf will throw an awful lot of weight onto that saddle when it hits the end of the rope. If his withers are round and low, you'll have to girth the saddle tight enough to keep it from slipping up on him.

When you do that, it's probably too tight for him to run the way he should. And it'll rub his hair the wrong way. A saddle girth that's too tight—like it's apt to be on a low-withered horse —will roll the horse's hair up until it hurts him and he won't work the rope. It'll be pulling his hair the wrong way. So you want good withers on a roping horse.

A horse has to have good hips and stifle, if he's going to get his hindquarters under him when he stops. But it's his forelegs that take the punishment when he stops that calf.

Look at the picture of the calf coming to the end of the rope. The horse's forelegs are set out there like a brace on a fence. The jar is going right down his forelegs. That's why, if he's weak or crippled any way in front, he can't take much hard roping. A horse that's weak in front can't stop good.

Starting His Training

You can start training a pony for a roping horse by the time he's a two-year old. But about all you'll want to do up to that age is give him an idea of what you want from him. Generally, you won't start any heavy training until the horse is at least two, and almost three. I don't like to enter a young roping horse in very many contests or rodeos even as a three year old.

To start him out so he won't dislike roping is important. The main thing is don't overdo anything. Don't let him go full speed after a cow or calf. Don't work him long at any one job the first few days. Don't try to stop him too hard on too many big calves.

What I like to do when I start a pony for roping is get him in a pen and let him trot around after some little calves that won't do much. Calves that weigh maybe 150 pounds or so. This way you can show the horse the "short cut" to reach those calves.

If one of them ducks to the left, show the horse how he can cut to the inside and catch the calf easy. Practice cutting to the inside of a circling calf, and the horse will start to gain distance pretty fast.

You can be swinging a rope while you're doing this. You can pitch the rope down on the ground in front of him, lay it up on his head, down over his neck—just make sure you don't hit the pony with the rope so it hurts him. If you do hit him much, he'll get the idea that rope is apt to hurt him anytime he sees it.

You want him to get the feel of it so that he won't fear it. Make a loop and hook it over his rump, for instance.

It won't be but a couple of hours before the horse will get used to the rope. Later, when you start swinging it as you chase a calf, the horse won't pay any attention to it.

Every day you might want to run four or five calves, as you get started. You wouldn't want to run each one more than a minute. This could take as long as half a day because you need to work into this a little at a time.

Chase a calf maybe a minute. Go at whatever speed the calf goes. Then pull the horse up and ride him around in a big circle. Ride him into the chute, pet him, get off him, talk to him, loosen your cinch.

"You want him to get the feel of it so that he won't fear it."

You're letting him rest this way and think about what he's just done. Pretty soon, he thinks about rest when he sees that chute and he won't mind it. If you start him off by doing nothing but running him out of that chute, it won't be but a half dozen starts before he won't want to go in there.

Now after some rest and a lot of fooling around, ease him into chasing another calf. This is a mighty important time and you don't want to rush things. It's better to go slow right at the first and waste a few days than to push a pony into things he's not ready for.

You haven't roped any calves off this horse yet and you sure don't want to—not until the pony is running calves good, stopping right and knows how it feels to have a heavy weight on the other end of that rope from him. The next thing is to give him the feel of the weight.

Pulling A Weight

The first time a horse stops a calf on the end of a rope it scares him. Which is only natural. It gives the horse a jerk. That's why you need to get the horse ready for it by making him pull a heavy weight and learn to work that rope.

You can tie your rope to a railroad cross tie or a log about 10 inches thick, and maybe six feet long. Just so it weighs about 150 pounds. Then put a jerk line on your saddle. This is a piece of heavy cord that you can run through a pulley on your saddle and is tied to his bit. Then you can pull on his bit and make him go back when you're out in front of him.

First thing I like to do when I start this is ride the horse up to that weight, then around it until he gets used to the thing. Then after I've tied the rope from the saddle horn to the weight, I back him almost to the end of the rope—to where there's not more than a couple feet of slack.

Then I get off and stand in front of him, holding the jerk line. I like to be about halfway to the weight. Then if he gets scared and breaks to run, I can just step on the weight to stop him. Step on the end and it'll stick in the ground.

Without any notice, then, you booger him. Make some sudden move with your hands so he'll jump back and put pressure on that weight. When he sees the weight move, it's apt to scare him. That's why you need to be ready to add your weight to whatever he's dragging. And it's a good thing too if you do this in a closed pen or arena.

Not every horse will go back against that rope like you want him to.

But you have to get him to do it—it's what helps get his withers tough and teaches him not to be afraid of that calf hitting the end of the rope. The jerk line will help you get him back.

Even a horse that has been taught to back like he should may not want to hit the rope hard.

If this happens, pull up some slack in the rope—between the

horse and the weight—then toss the slack at him to see if he'll take it up. Don't do this much. Pitch it at him a few times, until he finds that when he gets back against the rope—and takes up the slack—you won't do anything more with it.

Then if he starts working back against that weight, add some of your weight to it and tell him *"Whoa."* The more you make him think he's doing, the more he *will* do.

It wouldn't hurt to work him on this weight an hour or so every day for a week. And it's good exercise for older horses too. Helps tune them up.

But be sure to teach the young horse to keep the rope up off the ground, and keep the slack out of it. He should know how it feels on both sides of his neck too. Don't train him with it on the right hand side for a week, then put it on the left. Let him drag that log a couple of times on the right, then a couple of times on the left.

If you stand about halfway down the rope to the weight, he

"Put a jerk line on your saddle."

"Then you can . . . make him go back when you're out in front of him."

should drag it right to you. Some horses will catch on real quick and will knock you down with that weight if you're not careful.

Training To Stop On A Dime

When you start to train the pony to stop, like a roping horse has to do, you should know about where the horse likes the saddle on him. If the saddle is too far back, the horse just won't work a rope right. The saddle should be well up on his withers. You need plenty of padding—two inches of saddle blanket wouldn't be too much to start with. And if you plan to do much roping you need a saddle with a roping tree. They're built a little different.

Some call it the Quarter Horse tree. They're low in front but with a lot of clearance so there's enough hollow space under the front to protect the horse's withers.

Now if the pony is a well-broke Quarter Horse he already knows something about stopping. What you have to teach him here is timing, getting set for that weight to hit the end of the rope as he stops, then keeping pressure on the rope.

The signal for him to stop is the first step. One part of that signal is the slack in your rope that you throw by his head. If you were on him, roping a calf, throwing that slack out front of the horse would come right after you'd put the loop over the calf. It would be the horse's signal to put on the brakes. Another part of that signal would be you shifting your weight over into the left stirrup as you get off.

So that's what you teach him now: The slack thrown by his head and your weight shift—this should tell the horse it's time to stop.

To start with, just lope him down a fence. Pitch the coiled rope out in front of him. Pick up on the reins pretty firm, catch the horn in your right hand and start down off of him.

He may not stop all the way until your foot hits the ground. That's why you want to rein him sharp the first time you try this, and keep a good hold on that horn. It'll take him a few stops to get the idea. Later, he'll stop with no real use of the reins at all.

By the end of your first or second work period, he should know what you want and should be stopping by himself when you give him the slack-toss and weight-shift signal.

Here's a few things to remember about this: If you keep him stopping along a fence line, he won't have room to booger away from you. And as you get off, don't turn your toe in and jab him behind the foreleg. This will make him jump for sure. Ride him well forward. He'll carry you easier with your weight up over his withers.

Don't practice stops in the same place every time. If you do, he's apt to start "setting up"—that is, stopping before he should. After three or four stops in the same place, he'll figure that's right where he should stop from now on.

Stop him from a slow gallop and not a trot. You won't ever do much roping from a trot. In the gallop, make sure he's not running cross-legged as you go to get off. That's when he's leading with his left front foot and right back one. It's kind of rough riding and you won't like it much.

He needs to have all of his feet under him just right before you throw out the slack. If he stops in one smooth, short slide—and digs up ground doing it—the horse is coming right along.

A horse without a natural stop can be pretty rough. He may start down, raise up, come down and jab his forelegs in the ground two or three times. You won't win at many performance contests on this kind of horse, but he can be trained to jerk cattle just as hard as anybody's horse. You'll find some horses have a stop born in them and will stop like a dead end street.

How good your horse's stop gets can depend on how good your timing is, too. You'll get to know the horse's swing in a gallop after awhile, and you should get in the habit of signalling for a stop as his hind feet go under him. This gives you a short, deep skid, the horse's rump well down, with the forelegs braced to take the shock of that calf or cow hitting the rope.

"Pitch the coiled rope out in front of him."

"Later he'll stop with no real use of the reins at all."

This stopping practice is something else you need to do now and then to sharpen up any roping pony, no matter how old he is. And the practice won't hurt the rider any, either. Lots of young ropers get off so fast the horse doesn't know when the rider leaves him.

Putting The Rope To Work

When you've got the horse stopping and getting back on the rope, you can take him into a roping pen or arena and try him out on a few small calves. You may want to start from a chute or you may want to just pick out a calf and run him before you rope.

If you're not an experienced roper, be sure to pull the slack up with your right hand the minute the loop settles over the calf's head. You have to take up that slack or the calf will go right on through the loop. And you want to train that pony to keep running until you toss out that slack. There's lots of horses

101

don't do it. They're good roping horses and some people win on them. But they stop so fast that a lot of ropers can't use them.

The horse is not supposed to stop when you throw your loop. If he does, your loop may fall short. But he *must* stop when you throw the slack, after you have roped the calf.

Don't be surprised if—as you're getting that calf down—the horse drags the calf (and you too) a couple of yards. A horse that's spooky enough to make a good roping horse will do that. It's because you're making fast motions with your arms and hands.

You've been making motions with your hands for him to get back all this time. Now you're doing it again and he thinks you want him to back some more.

You ought to rope maybe three or four calves a day like this for about three days. They shouldn't weight much over 150 pounds if he's under three years old, and a medium size pony. If he's a full-grown, stout horse—14 to 15 hands high—it won't hurt to rope a cow or two to start with. They'll scare the horse but they won't hurt him—unless you keep doing it all day. Roping cows will sure make your horse get his feet under him.

Goats are good to start a roping horse on too because they'll teach him to be on the job. A goat won't run very far before he'll duck. In fact, you almost can't get a goat to run straight far enough to rope him. You'll rope most goats in a turn.

Here's some more "don'ts" for the first calves you rope off a horse you're training:

When you rope a calf and throw it down, it'll kind of spook the young horse—so I like to have a helper around to get the rope off the calf right away. Don't *you* ride up to that calf and let the slack all pile up in front of the horse while you untie the calf.

You've been trying to teach him to keep the rope *off* the ground. If you're working alone it's better to slip the rope off your saddle horn, after you've roped and tied the calf. Then go tie the horse to a fence and come back to untie the calf.

The reason I like to do that is because a horse will learn fast enough to stand there, get interested in watching you wrestle that calf and not give you any help on the rope. You go stacking that rope up knee deep in front of him and he'll think maybe that's all right anytime. He'll get so he'd just as soon be grazing with the calf tied to him as not. In fact, I've seen them do that at rodeos. This can get both embarrassing and expensive. I don't mind being embarrassed a little, but I sure do hate for it to be expensive!

Chute Training

Like I said earlier, if you're training your roping horse just for stock and ranch use, you won't need to worry so much about every little thing a horse may do. If he can help you stop a cow or calf and keep the animal down for a little while, he's done his job.

But if you expect to win rodeo money or Quarter Horse performance points, you have to pay mighty close attention to seeing that your horse gets a full education—and knowing how to get out of a chute is part of it.

The main thing is to train the horse not to leave that chute until you're ready for him to leave it. He shouldn't break when a gate rattles or opens or when the calf comes out. He should be quiet and ready and braced to go at *your* signal. Not before.

First thing a roping horse does is get nervous about that gate. He knows the calf is coming out and he can't wait to go after it. But if he breaks the barrier before the calf gets to the starting line, you'll have 10 seconds added to your time as a penalty. (I can't stand that. Takes me too long anyway.)

Now, of course, he'll get all happy wanting to go, so you have to train him by turning a calf out every so often, but not letting him run it. Have somebody rattle the gate, nod your head and say "let him go" but then hold him. Let the calf run on down the arena.

Next time, run the calf, and if the horse does what you want, pet him to let him know he did right. I wouldn't run over two to three calves the first time I put a horse in a chute.

Another thing. You'll be surprised how still a horse can stand in a chute when you're not spurring him. Lots of cowboys nod their heads and their feet just naturally go together. Any horse will go when you spur him, so don't do it—not until you're ready to go, as the calf passes the starting line.

Some horses don't like for you to hold them real tight in that chute. That makes them want to go more. So teach them to stand there on a loose rein. When you are about ready to go, pick the reins up, put a little tension on them and nudge him just a little with your heels. Pick his head up some so that the bit is a little tight in his mouth when he starts.

Maybe you wonder why. Well, if a horse could break faster with his head plumb loose, they wouldn't have bridles on race-horses. They'd let them run with a rope around their necks. Your horse will break faster with just a little bit of tension on that bit.

Some horses just won't like that chute. But a pony shouldn't be whipped and fought in the chute. Don't get mad at him because he wants to go, and tries to break before you're ready. When you started roping, you wanted out too, most likely. I've seen old time ropers a lot harder to keep in the chute than their horses ever were.

You can figure that about three things are apt to happen to a horse you're training in the chute, at one time or another.

He'll want to get too close to one side or the other. He may try to rub your leg against the chute, or he'll get the idea he wants to turn around about the time you ask for your calf. It's a little hard to see which way a calf has gone when you're sitting there looking the other way.

You can break a horse of hugging or rubbing one side of the chute by lots of practice in standing right and breaking right. With this turning around business, you have to show a horse real quick that it doesn't pay.

Some horses will stop that if you make them run the calf anyway. I once had a little horse I called Doodle that was this way. I had him in a rodeo at Cranfills Gap, Texas, one time when he was still pretty silly in a chute. He could have a fit quicker than you could think. On my first calf, I had him set about as good as I was going to, I reckon, when I asked for the calf.

When the calf came, Doodle turned around and hung both front feet over the back of that chute and I was pretty sore at him, but I tried to laugh and I did make him run that calf. And he ran every one after that. Of course, me and him had a little conference the next morning. I whispered in his ear a lot of things. And we won first on the next three calves.

But not all horses catch on this fast. Some need to be turned around in the chute until they're sick of it.

Once you ride your horse in the chute and face him toward where the calf will come out, you don't want him to turn around. If he tries to turn to the right a couple of times, go ahead and let him go that way—but keep him going. Turn him around until he begins to stagger, then stop him. You won't do that many times before he won't turn around.

This is a lot better than whipping your horse.

You'll find a lot of chute-crazy horses among those that can't run real fast, especially, because they've been whipped too much. A rider might hit the pony with the rope going into the chute, to get the horse stirred up. Then the horse would get hit again, coming out of the chute, to make him run faster. Pretty soon the horse would figure out that he was going to get hit one way or the other, or both. He wouldn't have any choice, and he'd just say to himself: "He's going to hit me with that rope *anyway* so I'm going to get a little bit of revenge." That's when a horse will give you trouble for sure.

You can help a horse break faster from the chute by finding out which way he stands the best. I've found that more than half of all roping horses I've ridden broke faster when I quar-

"Some need to be turned around in the chute . . ."

"You can help a horse break faster . . ."

tered them a little, instead of facing them straight down the arena.

Face him straight to start with, but then try him angled to the left and then to the right. Keep breaking him out of the chute until you find the way *he* wants to stand. That's how he'll break fastest, and it won't be long before that's how he'll stand every time.

Of course, you don't want to back the pony so far into the chute that he's pushing against the wall or fence. He can cap his hocks and hurt himself when he takes off. If his foot slips, the fence can skin him bad—next time he won't want to get back in the chute like he ought to. He won't really know what happened, but he knows something in that chute hurt him.

When riding a horse into the chute, also, I'd rather turn him toward the calf. But you'll find some that won't want to turn that way. So I think it's best to let him turn the way that fits him best. Just urge him into the chute and he'll most likely have a way it seems natural for him to turn—and even to stand.

It might not fit you, but if it turns out that *he* can start best that way, let the horse be satisfied. He's the one that's got to catch the calf first.

Rider Skill

How good you rope and ride, naturally, will have a lot to do with how fast your horse will learn and *what* he'll learn. You sure need to rope on him enough so that he knows how you operate. If you're consistent and don't miss a lot of calves, and if you do the same things every time, he'll be consistent too.

If you go to getting off him on the left this time and the right next time, he won't know what you're going to do next. He'll get as mixed up as a bowl of spaghetti and meatballs. He needs to know which side you're going to get off of. This is one reason why a left-handed roper needs to train his own horse. A left-handed roper pulls his slack from a different side and ropes from a different side. And the weight of the calf hits the horse a different way.

Of course, I know you're going to miss calves now and then. Everybody does. And a horse has to get used to you fishing for a calf—that is, throwing your loop at one you either can't see or else aren't sure you can reach. He has to know how it feels too, if you rope a calf off to one side and the calf jerks him while he's still in a turn. The pony's supposed to work to the end of that rope—no matter where the calf is. You can't figure to position the calf just right every time in a contest.

Naturally, the best thing for a young horse is to rope the calf while you're going straight down the arena—and try to rope it as near the same way as you can every time.

You may run into some things, though, that you can't do much about. One horse I used to have had the habit of fainting. Or at least he looked like he was fainting. When the neck rope got too tight, he'd just fall over. I was riding him in a match roping the day I found out about this.

I'd roped a calf and was tying it when I felt the rope go slack. I looked around and saw that horse had keeled over like a sick man. I ran back to him and got the rope off his neck and he staggered to his feet.

Just then some fellow called out and asked what was the matter with my horse. This struck me as kind of funny, so I hollered back that I usually tied the *horse* down *too,* but didn't have but one string with me that day.

If you plan to do much roping, in fact, you might get yourself some answers ahead of time to what you'll be asked about your horse. Some unusual things are going to happen to anybody who does much contesting.

When I was training this same horse, (the one that used to faint) I found out right away he wouldn't work a rope right, but I went ahead (because I couldn't afford *not* to!) and did some rodeo roping on him.

I did think up some excuses to go with him, though.

Sure enough, I was tying my calf down in a contest a little while later, when the rope went slack and this old horse comes walking right up behind me while I'm trying to tie that calf.

A friend of mine, Henry Savage, was the flag man, and he came over and said "Sikes, what's the matter with that horse?"

"Henry," I told him, "this horse is nearsighted."

"Well, I never heard of that. How do you know?"

"Because he has to get right over me to see what I'm doing."

Setting-Up Horses

Most of your good calf ropers nowadays are younger boys and practice a lot to see how fast they can leave the horse once they have put a loop on the calf. Only trouble with this is that the faster you leave a horse, the sooner he'll quit stopping good and working good. They'll stop before you even throw your rope. That's the bad thing about "setting-up" horses.

". . . younger boys practice a lot to see how fast they can leave the horse . . ."

This kind of horse will run to a certain spot and stop. If you're close enough to rope the calf, okay. If not, it suits him just the same—he doesn't have anything but a few oats invested. He'll run out there and stop and that's as far as he's going. You have one chance. If your rope doesn't take, it's plumb out of his mind to go any further.

I think the best policy is to train your horse to keep running until you rope your calf, pull your slack and throw it by his head. When he sees the slack, as I said before, he's supposed to stop.

He should be getting his hind feet under him good by the time the calf is at the end of the rope. You ought to leave him as you see that calf start over backward.

In ranch roping you sure don't want to leave your horse in much of a hurry because he's going to need your weight to stop a cow or steer that weighs almost as much as the horse does.

It's not so bad on Brahman cows. They'll run with their heads up higher than their body. On a 1,000 pound Quarter Horse, you can jerk down most any 1,100 pound Brahman cow—with *your* weight added to the *horse's*. Running with her head up, the cow gives you extra leverage. The Quarter Horse squats low and down comes the cow.

But not a big Angus cow. You'll break everything but the record if you rope one of them down around the neck and try a sudden stop. They're stout and heavy, don't have much neck and they keep their heads down. I've broken ropes on Angus calves that weighed only 350 to 400 pounds.

Young ropers these days are used to light calves—and that's the way it has to be. Years ago, a rodeo producer would drive up a bunch of fat calves weighing up to 400 pounds. He'd use them a day or two, then get fresh calves. Now they can't afford that, beef cattle being priced the way they are. And he wants smaller calves too because he wants to show how *fast* a man can rope and tie a calf—not how *long* it can take him. I've been to a few rodeos in past years where it was more like an endurance contest.

But this doesn't mean your horse can't use your weight—even if the calf only weighs 200. So I'd stay with him until the calf hits the end of the rope.

Then, by the time you get half way down the rope to the calf, your horse is up and started back.

Overwork

I think there's been a lot more horses—good horses—overtrained or overworked than those not worked enough.

Maybe you've seen this happen: Some fellow will come up to a roper and say "Let me see you rope two or three on your horse." Then somebody will want to see him rope two or three more. That can stretch out to too many calves.

You should quit when your horse is doing good. It's like throwing a ball to a kid. If he misses three or four times, he'll run and get the ball. But you keep him at it too long and he won't care about getting it any more.

A man can get a roping horse going good and he gets to enjoying himself more than the horse. The man may not know when to quit. More especially the younger boys.

In fact, one horse isn't enough for a young roper who's just starting and wants to learn pretty quick. He needs an old practice horse and one, younger, that he's training. He might want to use the older horse to practice his rope work on. Of course, for tying practice, you can just put a calf on the ground, grab his leg, jump over him and work from there.

A horse gets fed up with doing that over and over again. He may keep going but he won't be near as interested after three or four calves as when he started. I'd say 5 or 6 calves should be a limit for one practice roping session.

The Horse Learns Faster Than We Do

Don't be in too much of a hurry to make your pony a finished

"You should quit when your horse is doing good."

roping horse. He'll learn faster what he has to know than most people could.

In fact, I'm sure that if you started an untrained Quarter Horse with a man who'd never done any roping, that horse would be finished learning before the man got started good.

The horse isn't smarter. He's just learning one thing and he doesn't have much else on his mind. Besides, he was bred to be able to do that job.

I've seen this happen—I've seen a Quarter Horse that's been roped on 60 days, ridden by a roper with 10 or 12 years roping experience. I've seen that man rope four calves and make more mistakes than that young horse. There's all kinds of mistakes that a man can make.

Here's the kind you hear about most:

"...if I hadn't dropped my pigging string..."

"...if I'd a just got it on the calf's foot right..."

"...I missed my slack..."

"...if that calf would a fallen like he's *supposed* to..."

"...I missed his leg when I reached for it..."

"...I missed my rope when I started down there."

The roper can come back with half a bushel of "ifs"... (and I've made up my share of them) but the horse can't.

The Future Of Roping

You read now and then about how there's fewer cowboys and horses and how one of these days everything on ranches will be done on wheels. Then I guess a roping horse won't be of much use. But when I read where machinery is about to take over, I remember a rodeo I went to once in Pleasant Mound, Texas, outside of Dallas. Fellow named Jim Roy put it on every Saturday night and he liked to do different things to please the crowd.

He decided one time to put on a Jeep roping contest. He put a sack of cottonseed hulls on the hood of a Jeep, then put a saddle on that and buckled it down to where the saddle would stay. There were six of us that paid an entrance fee to rope off that Jeep.

We found out first thing that, from a standing start, the Jeep couldn't catch any of the calves across that short arena. So we put the Jeep back in an alley and gave it a running start on the calf. Then the driver would start the Jeep, call for the calf and one of us on the hood would get set to rope. If the calf went straight it wasn't any trouble to rope it. If the calf cut one way or the other, we couldn't. It was a pretty good chore to get off too. Most of us used our heads, though. Stuck them in the ground the first few times.

But we got the hang of it after awhile, and the Jeep actually jerked some calves down and managed to get in reverse to work the rope like a horse. The people got a kick out of it and after I tied a calf in 16:2 I got to enjoying it myself. It had me almost wanting to trade in my horse for a Jeep. But then I thought of something.

I would have had to hire a driver.

9 TRAINING THE BARREL RACER

Barrel racing is one of the newest things people are doing with Quarter Horses. Go to just about any good-sized rodeo or western horse show in the country and you'll see either women or children running the barrels. Usually at rodeos they do it for money. At shows, it's for ribbons and Quarter Horse performance points.

It's something they can do that's fun and safe. And it's a good test for a horse. You can sure find out what kind of speed and action a horse has got when you run the barrels with him.

Barrel racing started getting big pretty soon after World War II. Lots of high school rodeos picked it up because you don't have to be a good horseman—and you don't have to have a real fine horse—to just run the barrels for fun. And you don't need much but three oil drums and some open space to put on a barrel race.

But it got so popular and the barrel racers started getting so good that now—if you figure to win much at the big shows—you *do* have to be a pretty fair rider. And you sure *do* have to have a good horse.

How It Works

The idea, as you can tell from the diagram, is to see who can run circles around those three barrels and get back to the finish line the quickest.

You put the barrels 40 yards apart. They can be empty 55-gallon oil or gas drums. The first one should be 25 yards from the starting line. And you need 10 or 15 yards of space to the sides of each of those barrels, so you'll have room to go around.

You start the race on a dead run, when the nose of your horse crosses the starting line. You go around the first barrel to the right. Then around barrel number two to the left.

Go around that last one down yonder to the left too, then head for home fast as your horse will go. The clock stops when your horse's nose gets to the finish line. There ought to be 40 yards of stopping space behind the finish line so you can go full speed on past the end there.

If you go around a barrel the wrong way, or knock one over, they'll flag you out. You're disqualified for that go-around and they don't keep your time.

Sometimes you can come back for another go-round in the same rodeo or show, to get in on the "average." For instance, in some High School shows they'll just put a 10 second fine on you instead of flagging you out. But in most barrel races you

115

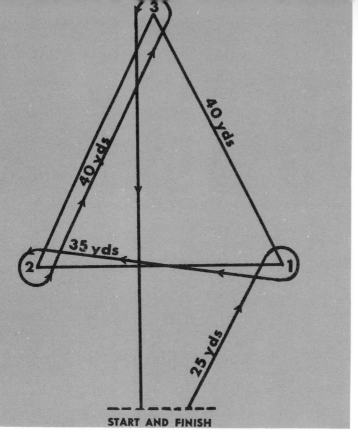

START AND FINISH

Barrel Racing Pattern

better figure on being disqualified if you knock over a barrel.

A go-round, as I've said before, is one time around for everybody. How many go-rounds you get depends on how many days the horse show or rodeo lasts. You'd get at least three go-rounds in most five-day shows, I'd say.

Of course, every barrel race everyplace won't be run just the same because all the arenas aren't the same size. If you don't have room for 40 yards between barrels, for instance, everybody there will have to get together on a shorter space. Usually you'll cut the distances down five yards at a time.

To get the best time, you want your horse to go straight to each barrel, and as close to it as you can without hitting it. If you hit one with your shin, you'll think it's full of rocks.

How It Got Started And Why

I'd say barrel racing came mostly from two things—flag racing and cowboy's wives who got tired of just watching rodeos.

116

I saw my first flag races back in the 1930's. It was a woman's and kid's event. They had a barrel at one end of the arena, bottomside up, with a bucket of dirt on it. You rode down there with a flag, stuck it in the dirt and grabbed the one that was there. Some places put a bucket with a flag on each side of the area. You'd have to go around after them all, then race to the finish.

The idea was to make the rider do something, same as the horse, and still go at full speed.

The cowboys' wives at rodeos liked the idea of doing something instead of watching all the time. So the barrel race got started—now you'll find a cowboy who'll use his horse to rope on, and then his wife will use the same horse to run the barrels.

And every year the Girls Rodeo Association picks a world's champion barrel racer just like the men do with calf ropers and bulldoggers. Boys and men run the barrels too in some places where they've started barrel racing clubs.

But it's one event where I think women have just as good a chance as men. Maybe better. You go out and pick ten good horsemen and I'm just not sure they could beat 10 women who know how to run the barrels. Those women *try*. They try like they weighed a hundred pounds.

What Horses Think Of It

Horses can get crazy about barrel racing. Fact, they'll get plumb foolish over it. Right away, they get to wanting to go—just like a racehorse—and outrun that stopwatch. I've seen a man have to lead lots of barrel racers into the arena by the bit and hold them until their time to run.

Some good barrel racers will get so they can run the race by themselves. Just like a reining horse will get to know the pattern in that event.

I owned one barrel horse I sold to a man in Palestine (Texas) who let a girl ride him. Her hat blew into her face going around that first barrel. She dropped the reins, but the horse ran the other two barrels anyway, and in good time too.

Now I don't mean that *all* Quarter Horses make good barrel racers. They're like football players. Some like the game and some don't. Those that don't—well, if the horse keeps making the same mistakes over and over, you may as well work him at something else.

What You Want In A Barrel Racer

If you don't care about the time it takes, you can run the barrels on any sort of pony. And have a lot of fun doing it.

But to win much now means you have to have a good bred horse and one that's trained for the job. I heard some pretty good advice not long ago from one of the best barrel race riders in the country, Mrs. K. Lee Williams, of Horatio, Arkansas. Here it is:

"I like a smaller horse for the barrels. Say, about 1,000 pounds. I don't like a horse with a long stride because he may not hit that stride just right—if he turns here, he'll hit the barrel, yet one more stride and he's too far past it.

"That's where you lose your barrel races—circling the barrels, and especially that first one.

"If you get a horse that's true, will go straight to the barrels and come around them pretty, he'll beat a horse that's just fast. Speed is wonderful if you can control it. But if you can't, it's a handicap."

I'll go along with Mr. Williams on something else too. Some of your best barrel horses are roping horses. Your roping horse has a good stop, he'll turn good and he'll run hard when you need him to.

Besides that, your roping horse can start winning for you right away, where it'll take you maybe two years to start a young horse from scratch, that's never been used for anything else.

Maybe that's why so many calf roping cowboys have got "a

good barrel horse that can flat run" they want to sell to some girl!

But I think it's true that the roping horse makes a better barrel racer than, say, a cutting horse. The cutting horse has the speed all right, but once he's trained for cutting, I'd think he'd be a long time picking up something so different—especially since there's no cattle for him to work *against,* in barrel racing.

Now about the sex of barrel racers. Since this event is mostly for kids and women, I wouldn't recommend stallions. They're sometimes unpredictable. You see lots of geldings used, and they're good where you're barrel racing just for fun. Geldings usually won't cost you as much—and you can also show them at halter if you want to enter some other event at a show. Geldings can be pretty unconcerned though.

Some women who do lots of barrel racing feel like mares make the best horses for this. The mare is more sensitive. And it doesn't hurt if your barrel horse is keyed up, wanting to go. It makes them a little bit more ready.

Anybody wanting mares instead of geldings or stallions would surprise some old time cow men. Lots of them wouldn't keep a mare on their place—not unless they were in the breeding business. Mares in the old days weren't to ride—just to raise more horses from. Now some of your best roping, reining, cutting and barrel racing Quarter Horses are mares.

Training The Barrel Racer

How you train a horse for barrels depends on what this horse has done before. If he's been used much for work on a ranch, he should be easier and quicker to train.

If you have a young horse that hasn't been used a lot, you may confuse him by walking or loping him around those barrels. He might get to thinking that's as fast as he's ever supposed to go.

A five year old roping horse wouldn't get that idea at all. You can put him in the pattern at a slow speed, then speed up

". . . be sure to run all three barrels, not just one or two."

as you get him to liking it. After he knows the pattern, I wouldn't run him through it fast more than three times in one day—and not oftener than every other day.

When he's built up some speed, try to make every run just like you'd do it if you were running in a show or rodeo. Keep other horses and riders out of the arena. Once you start the pattern, be sure to run *all three* barrels, not just one or two.

And if he makes what you think is a real good run, stop there, even it it's his first run that day. You want to stop after a good run, not quit after a bad one.

Don't forget that the first time you run at the show or rodeo is the one that'll count. They won't let you run a few for practice in the arena.

I'd think you'd want to train any barrel racer for six months before you enter him in a contest. If you try to rush the horse it may burn him out.

Now I don't mean you can take a two year old filly and be

doing much good at barrel races in six months. If she hasn't been used a lot, the big thing you'll have to teach that horse is to go around the barrels right and to turn on speed at the right time.

Take some of your old time roping or reining horses. They'll go to each barrel fast, do a sliding stop and a half rollback. Done right this is good, but if the rollback goes too far, you've knocked over the barrel.

That's why I think it's better to teach a young horse to run around the barrel, low and fast.

And again—be careful about letting a young horse lope or trot too much through the pattern at first. He *can* get the idea that he'll never have to go any faster through there. Once he knows the pattern keep up his speed every time you run a cloverleaf.

Conditioning Your Horse

Your horse has to be in shape to win much in this event. You can be sure the horse that beats *you* will be in good shape. And you don't have to be beat much in a barrel race. I've seen races where there was less than four-tenths of a second between the times of the first four horses.

One thing that's good for a barrel horse to do while he's in training is to work cattle. Do anything and everything you can. Open and shut gates, ride some pretty good distances, move cattle around.

Get him used to you and let him know he's a useful horse.

Then when you do get set to run the barrels, be sure your horse is fresh. Don't get him out behind the arena and work him half to death while you're waiting your turn to run. Warm him up easy but don't do much more than break a sweat on him.

You want him to do better than 18 seconds. If he runs much above that he may be putting on a good show but he's not making any money. An average of 17 ought to put you at the pay window or the ribbon lineup most all the time.

The Barrel Racer

Discipline

There's a time to spank your horse and lots of times not to. You can't expect to lay the bat to a pony *all* the time in any event and then expect that horse to give you all he's got.

If you watch many barrel races, you'll see girls whip their horses outside of the arena to see if they'll run, then inside the arena, all the way through the race. Your horse is probably scared anyway. Using the bat on him so much will burn him out. He won't want to go into the arena at all. If he likes the barrels, you can straighten out the things he does wrong.

A good rider knows where to hit a horse in a barrel race.

Some horses will take too long around a barrel. They'll sit down and hesitate. That's one place to use the bat—but only if your horse needs it.

The best thing to remember is that the less you whip a horse, the more he's apt to give you when you need it.

And you need to let your horse know when he pleases you. Won't be long before he'll *know* when he's pleased you and when he hasn't.

Then he can get to be a lot like you are. You get upset and he's upset. Your horse is apt to be just as calm as you are.

Safety First

Unless it's your turn to ride, the best place to be during a barrel race is outside the arena. When a good barrel horse gets into that last straightaway, he can move in a hurry. And you better tell the producer and everybody else to get out of the way because that horse won't recognize many faces.

At one barrel race I saw one time, they kept telling one of the show officials to keep clear of the alley where the horses went in and went out. He either didn't hear or didn't want to. Sure enough he turned his back at the wrong time and a girl rode her horse right down his back.

It didn't break any bones but it sure did bunch his ideas after that.

10 REINING AND OTHER PERFORMANCE EVENTS

Now we'll talk about the other show events where Quarter Horses can earn performance points: Reining, Western Riding and the Working Cowhorse.

These aren't easy for the horse because they amount to a cowhorse working without a cow. When you work cattle, your horse watches those cattle and takes his cue from them on some things he has to do.

But in these events, the horse takes his cue from his rider. Still, he has to have as much speed and control as if those cattle were all around him.

Diagrams in this chapter show the pattern for each event. You can see they're mostly combinations of things we've gone over in the first part of this book. In all of these events, your horse will need to rein good, have steady gaits and a smooth stop. He has to be able to back, roll over his hocks and pivot. He'll need to know figure eights and a change of leads.

Of these three events, more Quarter Horses enter the reining contest. This may be because you don't need much space to work out your horse, it's easy to stage, and it seems to have lots of appeal for youngsters and women riders.

REINING

You can tell from the diagram what this event calls for your horse to do. The pattern makes him run and stop, back, do two figure eights, rollbacks and pivots.

Not all Quarter Horse shows will use exactly this pattern, but most will come pretty close since it's what the American Quarter Horse Association recommends. It's a good stiff test for a horse—and rider too. Your horse is handled with just your reins—you're not supposed to handle him with legs or knees.

The event is run without using a tiedown on your horse. His head is loose. There are classes for both bitted horses and those with just a hackamore. Usually the hackamore class is the Novice class—for young horses.

In bit reining, you can use most any kind of grazing, half-breed or spade bit that fits the horse. Just so there's no chain or wire curbs or nose bands on the horse. Also you can't have any iron under his jaw.

With hackamore reining, you need four inches clearance between the horse's chin and the back of the hackamore—room enough for your hand to fit in there.

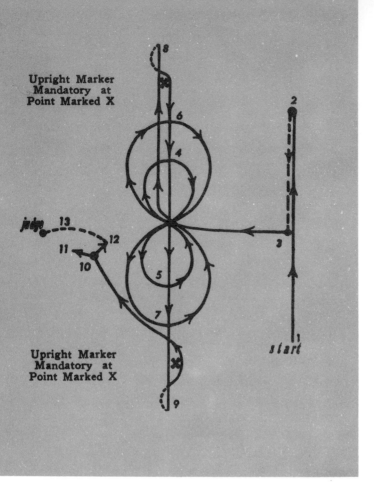

Upright Marker
Mandatory at
Point Marked X

Upright Marker
Mandatory at
Point Marked X

Reining Contest Pattern

That's to keep somebody from making a hackamore more severe than a bit. If you had a pony, say, you were afraid wasn't going to work right, you might want to put that hackamore way down on his nose with the back wrapped. They won't allow that.

As for the pattern, you shouldn't have to worry too much about not knowing what it is—not if the show officials do what they're supposed to.

A ring clerk has the job of letting contestants know ahead of time what the pattern is—in time for them to get used to it. Or, in some shows, a judge will have one man "set the pattern."

That man will ride it the way the judge tells him, so everybody will know what it's to be. At big shows, like Fort Worth, they may post the pattern a day in advance. This helps lots of new contestants who need some time to run through it—in case it's different from what they're used to.

Most of the big Quarter Horse reining shows are tough competitions. Let your horse open his mouth or bounce twice on a stop and you're probably out. Your horse can't wring his tail, stop crooked or break his gait, either—not without getting marked way down.

They'll mark the rider strict too. Change hands on the reins, grab the saddle horn, lose a stirrup or take the reins in both hands, and you've probably lost out for sure. You're not supposed to spur or quirt your horse in any way. At the smaller shows where you find younger horses and riders, you can make a few mistakes and still win. What we'll talk about here are the things to work hardest on to keep from making those mistakes.

Stopping And Backing

Most all Quarter horsemen who enter a lot of reining contests feel like a horse that can stop good is a horse that'll win for you. When your pony stops, he ought to scoop up some earth with his hind feet. He shouldn't bounce. It ought to be a smooth, straight slide, with his hind feet well under him and his forelegs braced. He needs to keep his head straight out and not up in your face. Next, you back him. When you start back, keep him going straight.

Pull the reins straight back toward your chest over the saddle horn. Tell the horse to "back" just before you put any pressure on the reins, then lean back a little in the saddle. You should rein back in short jerks followed by slack every time. Finally, he'll get so he'll back when you tell him to, without your having to pull much on the reins.

Rollbacks And Pivots

Not many things you'll do with a Quarter Horse look much better done right than rollbacks and pivots. But here's where good horses can get marked down right and left. These things may look easy but they take time for both you and the horse to learn.

One of the best rollback exercises I know for a horse is the one I talked about in Chapter 4—turning into a fence. Get your horse into a pen and run him down a fenceline. Stop and turn him into the fence all at once. He'll have to roll back to keep from hitting it. Later, when he learns to turn, keep him away from the fence. Make him turn in the open.

Another thing you'll want to work on is keeping your horse's body straight. It should be in line all the time. To keep it that way, put some tension on both reins, no matter which way you're turning.

In a left turn, say, keep a light pressure on your right rein, pulling at the same time on your left rein to start him in that direction. After you've trained him, you can have your reins pretty snug.

You don't want your horse turning his head while you're showing him, either. You'll see some horses that want to sling their heads to one side or the other. This marks you down pretty bad in most reining shows.

Changing Leads

Here's a place where you can cause your horse trouble if you don't learn right along with the horse. When a horse is on the wrong lead, in a turn, he can be hard to ride if you crowd him. He may be running one way with his front feet and another way with his backend. It's hard for him to turn that way. The rider will know about it too—it'll feel about like you were riding in a car where one tire has a big knot on it.

To see how well your horse changes leads, you'll have two figure eights to do in the reining pattern. Right here is where some horsemen make a mistake. They figure eight their horses too much in training.

Where the two circles of that eight come together is where

the horse should change leads. But if you keep riding your horse through one figure eight after another, he'll pretty soon beat you to the draw. He'll anticipate that change and he'll figure that all figure eights are that same size and that he's always supposed to change leads right there.

You ought to think of a figure eight as two circles that meet. Then you'd put your horse into one of those circles for maybe six or eight turns. Stop the horse. Now put him into another circle the other way.

You might want to remember this: A good reining horse should never need to know what you'll want him to do next.

Before you go into *any* figure eights, you ought to be sure that his leads are steady—that he's on a left lead in a left hand circle —(that is, leading with his left forefoot)—and on a right lead in a right hand circle.

You don't want to use any leg pressure to keep him on these leads but it's okay to put a little more of your weight onto your left stirrup when you're in a left lead, and the same the other way. As you shift a little to the left, the horse will work to keep under you. Horses don't like the weight on them to be off balance. So he'll tend to lead in whatever direction you shift your weight.

Once he leads to the left and right, you can put him into some figure eights. It'll take some horses a pretty good while before they'll change leads right there where the two parts of the eight come together. It's a good chore for a horse to do this at all. He's got to be a well-balanced pony. Even an old, well-trained horse gets mixed up now and then changing leads.

But it's good practice for any horse—cow ponies and all. And kids can learn a lot from knowing how to do a figure eight right. They learn how to balance themselves.

You just have to watch and see that the horse isn't overworked in the figure eight so that he starts setting up on you or getting too tired. Be sure your figure eights are round circles, not long and flat.

I'd say that four or five minutes at a stretch is the most you'd want to work your horse at this. Don't forget that two minutes is the time limit on the reining pattern in shows. If you get out and practice 15 minutes on eights, you can burn your horse out on them.

If you have an experienced horse, it'll take you about 30 days of regular riding and work to put him into shape for a reining contest. Speed is not so important in this contest as a horse's disposition. You'd want your reining horse to be a little calmer than most cutting horses, I'd think. But it's safe to say that 90 percent of trained cutting horses, with some extra work, can make good reining competition horses.

One more thing. Try not to ride your horse out of the arena after you finish the reining pattern. Either walk and lead him out or back him out. This is because a lot of reining horses will start watching the gate while they're working out there. You don't want this. You want the horse to keep his eyes in the center of the arena. Where his eyes go, his ears go. And where his ears go, his nose goes too. You can ride a roping, cutting or barrel horse out, but I wouldn't advise you to ride your reining horse out.

I do remember a roping horse I had once that I couldn't ride out of the arena, either. I'd start for the gate on him, after I'd roped a calf, and he'd go to jumping up and down like a salt shaker. So a friend asked me—"Sikes, you're a trainer—why don't you break him of that?"

I told the man the horse was 15 years old when I bought him. He was a good roping horse. He'd been lead out of arenas all his life. I figured I'd rather keep on winning on him than risk abusing the horse enough to make him change that one habit.

WESTERN RIDING

The diagram for this event shows you that your horse has to walk, trot, lope, go through gates, over small obstacles and back.

This is not a race. The idea is to show how well your horse can do as a ranch pony, going along trails or across country. He'll be judged on the quality of his walk, trot and lope; how he moves and does what you want him to; on his manners, disposition and sense.

This event doesn't call for much extra training if you have an experienced cow pony. Any Quarter Horse that's used to ranch work can be taught the pattern pretty easy. You'd want to work on his backing—even though there's only one back at the end of the event—and put him around the markers until he circles them smooth.

The obstacles he'll have to clear usually aren't high. They put them in just to break the horse's stride.

You can use a severe bit, and tie-down and wear spurs if you

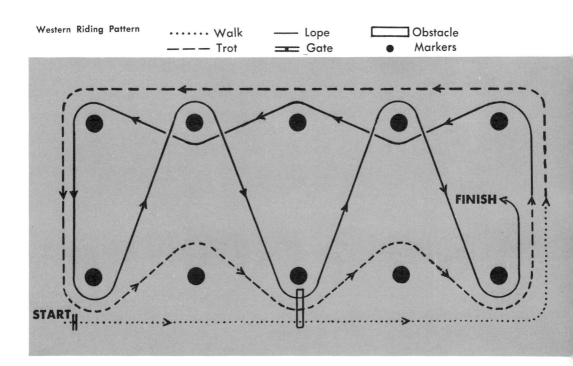

want to in most Western Riding events, but you may lose points with the judge if you use them too much. He'll be apt to think much more of the horse that doesn't need so much controlling.

WORKING COWHORSE

Here's another place ranch and roping horses can make performance points. It's a hard test for any using horse, if it's run right, but it's the kind of work ranch ponies do every day.

You'll have to walk, trot, lope and run your horse, do full stops, backs, bustaway turns and drag a heavy sack. The sack is supposed to represent a calf, cow or steer.

Your horse will be judged on his gaits, how he reins, his disposition and rope work. You're supposed to use stock saddle,

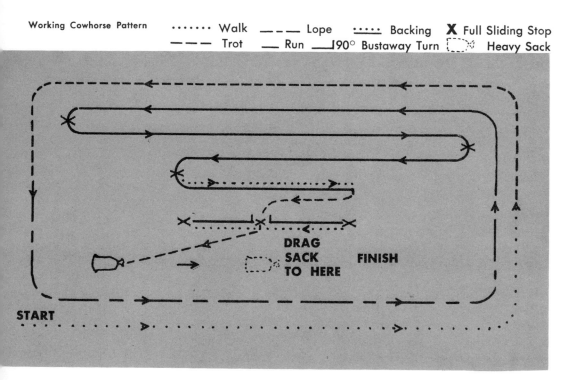

Working Cowhorse Pattern ⋯⋯ Walk — – — Lope ⋮⋮⋮ Backing **X** Full Sliding Stop
— — — Trot — Run —|90° Bustaway Turn ⌐⌐⌐ Heavy Sack

DRAG
SACK   FINISH
TO HERE

START

hackamore and rope, or curb bit. You can't use a tie-down, nose band, neck rope or other extra equipment.

The rope work is pretty important in this event. They put a rope around the sack—which is full of sand—and give you the other end. You loop the rope over your saddle horn and drag the sack for at least 25 feet. Then you turn your horse under the rope so the rope goes over his head, then around his croup. This is to show he's not rope shy.

Next you tie the rope to the horn, back the horse until the rope is tight, then get off. Walk down the rope to the sack. You can sit on the sack if you want to, but you can't make any signal to your horse. He's supposed to keep that rope tight and stand there quiet, with no rider.

11 THE HALTER SHOW

The halter show is where Quarter Horses are judged on the way they're built, not on what they can do. And you don't win much money at halter shows. You can win some, but mostly it's a contest between good-bred horses, and gives a contestant the fun and honor of proving how good his horse is put together —at least in the eyes of one judge.

The show gets its name from horses being shown with nothing on them but a halter. This event gets good crowds because it's also a place where breeders find out what judges think of the kind of horses they're producing. And people who may want to buy some horses get to look over the crop.

As you can see, the more halter shows your breeding stock can win, the more your horses are apt to be worth in the long run.

But I'd guess that lots of horse lovers don't enter a halter show with that in mind. The ones who enter geldings sure don't. It's just a good feeling to take your horse into a ring, have a judge look him over next to lots of other good horses, then find out he thinks yours is the best.

Now I'm not going to tell anybody they can win a halter show unless their horse deserves to win. But there's lots of things you can do to give your horse the best chance of winning. There's things like training for a show, good diet, grooming, and the behavior that contestants and horses both need to know before they step into a show ring. That's what this chapter is all about.

What The Judge Looks For

As a contestant, you first ought to know the things your horse will be marked on—either up or down—when he's in the halter show.

Here's how most judges will look the horses over:

One of the first things he'll see is how good your horse holds himself. He shouldn't be propped up on one foot. He should stand flat on all four feet. Sort of at attention, with the feet straight down from the shoulders in front and from the stifles in back.

The head should be up and so should the horse's ears. You want that horse's face to look awake because that's one of the first things every judge will study.

And he'll count off if the horse has a bad Roman nose or long ears or if he's too thick in the throat latch.

Next the judge will start from the ground and go up. If he doesn't have good feet he isn't a good horse. The judge won't like a flatfooted horse with no heel. He'll want to see a horse standing up on his feet. The foot should have a good wall to it and should be trimmed neat.

Then he'll see if the ankles are straight. Some horses have crooked ankles with knots on them. These can causes him trouble if the horse is used much. Around the knees, he'll look for splints. They're counted as a weakness.

"He should stand flat on all four feet."

The judge will want to feel the horse's withers and hips too. He won't want to see a mutton-withered horse—one that's flat across his withers, to where a saddle could slip off up over his head. Most judges will mark down heavy here. Poor withers, poor horse.

A judge won't use a tape measure but he knows how wide he wants to see your horse across the back. And how long from the hock to the pastern on the hindquarters. He'll mark off too if the muscling isn't what it ought to be on the inside and outside of those hind legs.

Now a scar won't make a lot of difference with some judges

if it doesn't hurt the horse's action. Some judges won't count off for scars and scratches if they can tell the horse got them working.

When you move your horse to and from the judge, he'll look to see how straight the pony goes. It'll count off if he slings a foot out, or swings one around, like he's mowing hay. A pigeon-toed horse will turn them in.

He's supposed to walk straight as a soldier on all four feet.

Any judge will count off for long-backed, hog-backed, or sway-backed horses. The hog-backed horse has a hump in his back right in front of his hips. I saw a friend with one like that in Louisiana not long ago. I had to tell him that horse was *bound* to have some Brahman in him.

Diet And Grooming

Before you get near the show ring, there's a few things you can do for your horse so he'll look his best to the judge.

One is to take any extra fat off that horse. You want him in good flesh for the halter show but not fat. A fat horse won't show his muscling like he should. This means you want to ride or exercise the horse almost every day for three or four weeks before a show. It wouldn't hurt to trot or walk him a couple of miles a day.

Don't be afraid to wash your horse. But not often. Not more than once a week. Wash him like you would a dog—with warm soapy water, and make sure you get all the soap off when you get through. Then keep a blanket on him, to keep his hair turned right.

This is also a good time to put raw eggs in your horse's feed to make his hide glossy. You can feed him about three raw eggs both night and morning. Mix them right in with his oats and bran, if that's what you're feeding. Eggs may be a little messy if the horse doesn't clean it all up, but the mess can be worth it. It'll sure keep a horse's coat glossy.

Then keep some kind of powder or fly spray around. Don't spray it right straight on your horse. Back away from him and let the mist fall all over. And don't put so much on the horse at once that it will blister him. You'd want to do that three or four times a day when the flies are bad.

If you don't keep this pony shod all the time, you should keep his feet trimmed. And don't try to make them look like *you* want them shaped. You're supposed to leave them natural. I'd trim his feet a couple of weeks before you plan to show him.

Just before the show, you can thin and shorten his tail and mane. He'll look wider through the hips with a short tail.

I think a horse's neck looks better if the mane is medium to short-cropped. Most barber shears will do the job, although I like an electric rig because it's faster and easier.

And you'll need a small pair of scissors to trim hair off the horse's face and nostrils.

With all this fuss made over him, your horse may feel so good he can't stay on the ground. That's why you need to make him train a little—so he knows what that show ring is all about.

Training For A Halter Show

Training a horse for this event doesn't take near the time or work you'd need to train a horse for, say, roping or cutting. Horses that have been used much do fine at halter shows because they're calm, well-mannered ponies, as a rule. It's the younger spoiled horse, the kind that isn't worked at anything, that kicks up a fuss most of the time.

What you need to teach your horse for a halter show is to lead good in the arena, stay awake with his head up about level with yours (if you're a grown person) and how to move and stop straight when you're showing him to the judge.

You do this by practicing what you'll go through in the show ring. Here's what happens in a halter show.

When you lead your horse into the ring with the others, you'll go in a circle around the judge and then line up. There'll probably be a ring steward in there with the judge to help get everybody straight.

The judge will look each horse over, one at a time. He'll have each contestant lead his horse away from the rest, then turn and come back toward him. The next thing he'll do is have each horse trotted off aways and stopped. As sharp a stop as you can make it from a trot. Then the horse is trotted back toward the judge.

After he's looked at each horse, the judge will wave it over to another line. The contestant is told where to put his horse. But it's too soon for you to know if you've won anything.

When the judge has finished looking at each horse one time, he'll know which three or four horses he likes most. Then he'll shift them around until he has them lined up the way he thinks they rate—first, second, third and so on. This can take a little while.

Sometimes you'll see a judge move a horse two or three times before he makes up his mind where to leave him in the lineup. A lot of judges do this and take their time about it. It can make some contestants nervous but a good judge will study the horses until he's sure he has them the way he thinks they ought to finish.

This gives you some idea of what goes on in the show ring. It ought to be enough to show you that your horse has to stand right, lead good and behave himself.

The best way to train him to do this is to do it—and not just one day before the show. Get your horse out in a pasture or in an arena and lead him at your side. Go at a walk, then a trot. Even a short gallop—if your wind is up to it. Go about 20 yards in a straight line, turn around and come back the same way. Turn him to the right one time, to the left the next. Stop your horse straight enough times so he'll know what he's supposed to do. If he doesn't keep straight when he moves or stops it could give a judge the notion that your horse is a little paddle-footed, when he's not at all.

Don't forget that your horse needs to keep his feet under him when he's still. He shouldn't be all stretched out. And when *he* moves, don't *you* move like you were dragging a log. You walk at attention and more than likely your horse will too.

If you just stroll along holding the end of that halter shank, your horse may take a notion to graze awhile. I've seen them do it.

Good Manners

Not just the horses but the contestants ought to know how to behave in a halter show ring.

First, the horse. It doesn't pay to spoil a horse in the first place. If you plan to show him at halter, you better make *sure* you don't spoil him.

It can be embarrassing, if you pet a horse and let him have his way all the time. You'll want *your* way when you get to that show, and it won't work. You'll expect him to stand there at attention like a soldier. He'll stand there like a four year old kid wanting some candy and mad because he can't have it.

I've seen them get loose and run off through all the other horses. Or you may have your horse lined up with the rest, nice and quiet, when he'll reach out and kick the horse next to him. You can imagine how big that goes over.

Or maybe a young stud will just up and walk off, dragging you with him. He can do it if he decides to. I saw one at Houston once that almost pulled a fellow out of the arena.

So you should have, on a stallion anyway, a halter you can manage him with. One that the horse fears enough to mind. I mean a halter with a metal nose band, so that you can slap him under the chin or on top of his nose if he won't behave. In fact, I think stallions in a halter show ought to *have* to wear one something like that.

If you have a quiet, good-mannered horse standing there and I lead up a horse that won't behave, you'd get mighty upset if my horse skins yours before you can get out of the way. And you'd have a right to be upset.

It seems like some people won't make a horse behave because they think so much of him. Or they're afraid somebody will think they're being mean to the horse if they make him be quiet.

"Stop your horse straight enough times so he'll know what he's supposed to do."

They may not be giving their horse a fair chance if they don't keep him in line. A judge isn't supposed to count off if a horse acts up, but it can sure be hard to show any judge what a fine pony you have with that horse jumping all over the place.

There's some things that judges don't like about contestants' manners too. First, you sure ought to be on time for the event.

And a judge won't like to see a contestant pick at his horse all the time, with a quirt or whip. You need to learn when to touch your horse and when to leave him alone.

Some contestants will try to hide a scar or a crooked foot by standing in front of that leg. Others will try and come up with all kinds of excuses—like "Oh, *that* won't hurt him," or maybe "He just did that in the trailer."

No judge likes contestants arguing with him after the event is already judged, either. After all, it's one man's opinion. The judge has picked the horses *he* liked. Nobody expects all judges to figure all horses just the same.

If you have a good horse, you'll win somewhere. Some judge will like him.

The thing I think every contestant can expect is that a judge should at least look his horse over. I know that sometimes it's a temptation not to.

Not long ago I judged a show where a boy had a horse I didn't know how to figure. At first I thought maybe the carpenters were fixing to *build* a horse. It looked like they had the frame up, anyway. But I hated to not look at the pony. It may have been the best horse that boy had. So I looked at the boy's horse. The horse didn't win anything, but next time I'll bet the boy shows up with a better animal. He knows now what he'll need to win, still he feels like he was at least *in* that show.

If somebody leads a *mule* in there, a judge is supposed to at least see what it is.

12 STRAIGHTAWAY RACING

Right now there are probably more "short races" being run every year, seen by more people, with more money bet on Quarter Horses, than ever before in this country's history.

But there's some good reasons why Quarter Horse people don't expect everybody to start wanting to race their ponies. It doesn't cost a thing to race your Quarter Horse across a pasture. But when you start entering horses at organized race meets, you're spending a good deal more money than you would just to take your horse to a halter or performance show.

What's more, the purses still aren't big. If a man has a number of Quarter Horses he can move from one track to another, he may break even—because some of those ponies will finish in the money if they're good horses to start with.

But take the leading money-earning owner of 1957, Donald K. Brokaw of Pico, California. The records show he had 10 horses working for him during the year and his total winnings came to $47,158. The top-winning Thoroughbred in 1956, Needles, made nearly ten times that much, all by himself. Quarter Horse purses in 1957 averaged only $933.

So people who race Quarter Horses are still doing it pretty much because they love Quarter Horses and can afford to take them to the short races. Some breeders figure, and rightly so, that winners will boost the value of their breeding stock. But most horsemen are also the kind who just have to *compete,* no matter what.

Time Is The Thing

The difference between Thoroughbred distance racing and Quarter Horse racing is more than how *far* the horses run. It's also *how* they run. It's like comparing a runner in a 100 yard dash to one who runs the mile.

That miler will start fast, then go into a long stride for three-quarters and finally end with all the kick he's got left. The dash man will run as hard as he can every minute he's moving. It's pretty much the same in horse racing.

That's why time on Quarter Horse tracks is so important. Distances have to be measured right down to the inch and times have to be measured electrically if you're going to have the right kind of quarter-mile races.

It didn't used to be this way. Back in the last century, these short races weren't very formal at most places. In the cow country, you'd see a lot of two-horse races—where one rancher would bet almost anybody *his* horse was the fastest.

Most western county fairs staged races too. They didn't have grandstands or professional jockeys like they do now. They'd try to keep the time at most places, but in lots of those early races the time wasn't nearly so important as who won. Plenty of land, and livestock would change hands after those race meets.

Just about every state started coming up with a horse that people called "the fastest Quarter Horse of them all." Names like Steel Dust, Copperbottom, Peter McCue, and Bob Wade got big reputations from the 1850's on into the 20th century. You could hear all sort of tales about how fast they could cover the quarter mile distance.

The fastest of them all, supposedly, was Bob Wade. An old time publication called Goodwin's Official Turf Guide says that Bob Wade ran 440 yards in Butte, Montana, August 20, 1890 in 21.25 seconds. It's hard to say now how accurate their timing was, but if that figure is right, Bob Wade must have been a mighty fine horse.

The present world record was set by a stallion named Go Man Go, in 1957. He covered the quarter in 21.8 seconds, and the speed was electrically-timed.

But if you get together with some owners and start talking about modern Quarter Horses being slower than the old timers, you'll probably get yourself a good argument in nothing flat!

It does seem likely that modern Quarter Horses would be better bred, trained and conditioned than any of the 19th century ponies—although some of those old western cow ponies had as much endurance as any horse could have. They were small horses, mostly—a lot would weigh less than 1,100 pounds and stand 14 hands high, or less. In those days speed wasn't so important as how long and how far your horse could carry you.

When the Thoroughbreds came to the Southwest, it gave those Mustang ponies longer legs and speed the cowboys wanted.

You won't find cowboys riding the best Quarter Running Horses these days at the big tracks, but you can be sure there's plenty of them in the grandstand watching.

World Records

Here is a list of modern Quarter Horse speed records for the different short races: (In some cases, several horses are co-holders).

Distance	Record Holder	Time	Year Set	Place
100 yards	Dolly Mack	6.1 Sec.	1947	Del Rio, Texas
220 yards	Bright Eyes	12.1 Sec.	1950	Tucson, Ariz.
	Tonta Gal	12.1 Sec.	1946	Tucson, Ariz.
	My Texas Dandy	12.1 Sec.	1947	El Paso, Texas
250 yards	Bright Eyes	13.4 Sec.	1950	Tucson, Ariz.
	Super Charge	13.4 Sec.	1954	Phoenix, Ariz.
	Monita	13.4 Sec.	1949	Del Rio, Texas
300 yards	Clabbertown G	15.5 Sec.	1951	Los Alamitos, Calif.
330 yards	Miss Louton	16.9 Sec.	1958	Denver, Colo.
	Miss Panama	16.9 Sec.	1948	Del Rio, Texas
350 yards	Double Bid	17.8 Sec.	1959	Los Alamitos, Calif.
	Pap	17.8 Sec.	1959	Los Alamitos, Calif.
	Clabber's Win	17.8 Sec.	1958	Pomona, Ariz.
	Go Man Go	17.8 Sec.	1958	Los Alamitos, Calif.
	Vannevar	17.8 Sec.	1958	Ruidoso, N. M.
	Woven Web	17.8 Sec.	1948	Los Alamitos, Calif.
400 yards	Double Bid	20.0 Sec.	1958	Ruidoso, N. M.
440 yards	Go Man Go	21.8 Sec.	1957	Ruidoso, N. M.

Chart 1—Grading And Qualification Standard

GRADE		220	250	300	330	350	400	440
						:17.8	:20.1	:22.0
				:15.5	:16.9	:17.9	:20.2	:22.1
REGISTER				:15.6	:17.0	:18.0	:20.3	:22.2
	"AAA"		:13.4	:15.7	:17.1	:18.1	:20.4	:22.3
		:12.1	:13.5	:15.8	:17.2	:18.2	:20.5	:22.4
OF		:12.2	:13.6	:15.9	:17.3	:18.3	:20.6	:22.5
							:20.7	:22.6
	"AA"			:16.0	:17.4	:18.4	:20.8	:22.7
MERIT		:12.3	:13.7	:16.1	:17.5	:18.5	:20.9	:22.8
		:12.4	:13.8	:16.2	:17.6	:18.6	:21.0	:22.9
								:23.0
				:16.3	:17.7	:18.7	:21.1	:23.1
	"A"	:12.5	:13.9	:16.4	:17.8	:18.8	:21.2	:23.2
		:12.6	:14.0	:16.5	:17.9	:18.9	:21.3	:23.3
							:21.4	:23.4
				:16.6	:18.0	:19.0	:21.5	:23.5
	"B"	:12.7	:14.1	:16.7	:18.1	:19.1	:21.6	:23.6
		:12.8	:14.2	:16.8	:18.2	:19.2	:21.7	:23.7
								:23.8
				:16.9	:18.3	:19.3	:21.8	:23.9
	"C"	:12.9	:14.3	:17.0	:18.4	:19.4	:21.9	:24.0
		:13.0	:14.4	:17.1	:18.5	:19.5	:22.0	:24.1
	"D"	:13.1	:14.5	:17.2	:18.6	:19.6	:22.1	:24.2

Chart 2—Weight Allowance

AGE	220	250	300	330	350	400	440	Allowance
							140	minus .3
				140	138	134	132	minus .2
4-year-olds	132	131	129	128	127	125	124	minus .1
and older	116	116	116	116	116	116	116	STANDARD
	100	101	103	104	105	107	108	plus .1
							100	plus .2
							136	minus .3
				136	134	130	128	minus .2
3-year-olds	128	127	125	124	123	121	120	minus .1
	112	112	112	112	112	112	112	STANDARD
				100	101	103	104	plus .1
						127	124	minus .3
			126	124	122	118	116	minus .2
2-year-olds	116	115	113	112	111	109	108	minus .1
	100	100	100	100	100	100	100	STANDARD

(As compiled by The American Quarter Horse Assn.)

Grading Qualification

When a Quarter Horse goes into a straightaway race, at a recognized Quarter Horse track, he's working for more than money. He—or his owner, anyway—is trying to earn performance points. When a Quarter Horse wins races at different distances, his performance is graded. If he runs fast enough, often enough, he may qualify for the AQHA Register Of Merit or—with enough halter show points—the title of AQHA Champion.

Naturally, you'd want to get into that Champion's bracket if you could. From 1940 through 1957, only 27 different Quarter Running Horses made that grade. They won good money, of course, but they also became worth a lot more and produced colts that could bring a better price.

Getting in the Register of Merit also makes your horse worth more, but (and I'd say this is even more important) it also helps get him "promoted" to a higher registry (from Appendix to Tentative, or Permanent) if he's not already there.

Performance points are awarded for racing at the end of every year. The AQHA takes a list of the best times for all the distances run and divides the AAA and AA horses into three groups. They try to make the groups the same size. Horses in the top group, with the fastest times, get six points toward a championship. The second group gets five points each, and horses in the lowest group get four points.

You need 30 points to earn the AQHA Champion title and your horse must run in the AA or AAA time to be eligible for Register of Merit.

Now this grading and qualification system will look hard to understand if you're a beginner, but stick with me and we'll ease through it. As you see from Chart 1, it's divided into six time grades—from D on up to AAA. The times you see under each distance show the leeway that's possible without dropping into the next lower grade. Naturally, the longer the race, the more time spread you have to allow a horse.

If your horse runs the 440 in 22.5, let's say, he's done it in AAA time. But if the race is run in 22.5 and your horse comes in *second* by two lengths, it's a different story. For grading purposes, his time would be 22.9 and that would be Grade AA. Here's why:

By this system, you figure a horse's grading time by adding one-tenth of a second for each half a length, (six feet or any fraction thereof) he finished behind the winner. If he was second by a whisker, you still add half a length, or one-tenth second, to his time.

You can figure this way for every horse in the race, no matter how far back he finished.

Take another case: Your horse was third. He was a length and a half behind the horse that finished second. The second place horse trailed the winner by three-quarters of a length. The winner's time was 18.2 at 350 yards.

The winner, of course, was AAA at 18.2. Horse number two, adding on two-tenths of a second, was AA at 18.4. Your horse, adding another three-tenths, would be graded at 18.7.

Maybe you're wondering why a horse that's second by just a nose has a full tenth of a second added to his time. This is so that a beaten horse will never get the same credit as the horse that wins.

As the chart shows, horses that run in AAA or AA time, are eligible for the Register of Merit—with a couple of *ifs*. The AQHA's Racing Division checks the records to see that the races were timed electrically, that the horses weren't pushed by a tail-wind, and that the horses carried the minimum weight. The Register of Merit can help a horse move up to the Tentative Registry if his blood line is approved.

Chart number 2 is what the race handicapper goes by to try and give each horse an equal chance to win. He'll want to adjust the weight each horse carries, measured against how fast each horse has run that same distance before. What the handicapper tries to do is to make every horse in the race finish in a dead heat. That won't happen, of course, but he's supposed to try.

First, he'll check each horse's record to see which one has run that distance the fastest. Then he'll add weight (lead weights are later put into the saddle) to the fastest horse, a little less to the next fastest, and so on down the line.

To give an example, we'll say there are four horses—each four years old—in a 440 yard race. The fastest horse has run it before in as little as 22.6. Another horse in the race has run it in 22.7, another in 22.8, and still another in 22.9. (Handicappers would sure be pleased if it always turned out so simple!)

Anyway, we'll say the handicapper decides that the fastest horse should carry 132 pounds. The time of the next fastest horse was one-tenth of a second slower. You'll see in the table, that this means he can carry eight pounds less, or 124 pounds. The third horse was another one-tenth slower, so he'll carry 116. The slowest horse, 22.9, would then carry 108 pounds.

In line with how fast they've run before, this should give each horse an equal chance to win that race.

This grading standard has been used by the Quarter Horse racing people since 1942. It's been changed a little from time to time as the horses kept running faster.

It has come a long ways from 75 years ago. They "timed" some races then by just watching to see which horse came in first.

13 BULLDOGGING

You won't find much of this going on at Quarter Horse shows.
It's a rodeo event, also called Steer Wrestling. The idea is for
a man to ride up alongside a steer going full speed, dive off his
horse onto the steer's neck, then make the steer fall flat by twist-
ing the head and horns around. He gets help from a hazing horse
and rider who come alongside to keep the steer going straight.

In case this doesn't sound easy, it's not. It can get pretty dan-
gerous, but rodeo crowds like it and there's always lots of boys
ready to try for top money at bulldogging.

Just about every bulldogging and hazing horse now is a Quarter Horse. Some aren't registered because a horse's breeding at rodeos isn't as important as how much he can help a man win. They don't give these horses any performance points, but I know of one oldtime bulldogging horse that's supposed to have helped win $1,000,000 in his lifetime.

That's why you'll find lots of good Quarter Horses dogging and hazing that are worth up around $2,000 and more, even though you'd have a tough time getting all the registration papers on them. A horse's value can sure change in a hurry, too.

One time I gave a friend a half-trained horse I didn't have time to work with, and I told the fellow the horse wasn't ready for much yet. But he was anxious and came back the next week. Said he wanted to do some bulldogging with that horse. He insisted, so I got on a hazing horse, put a couple of steers in the chute and here we came up the arena.

My friend wasn't going to jump at the first steer. He said he'd see how the horse would run. That little pony went right on by the steer just like he was supposed to. We pulled up at the other end of the arena and my friend said, "Sikes, I wouldn't take $500 for this horse."

I said, "He'll cheapen up some on that next steer."

So we went back to the chute, got ready and here we came again.

He leaned over to get down on that steer and that horse went all to pieces—he bucked, and got the man all up around his neck.

Finally he got the horse stopped, got off and said, "Why, you nickel son-of-a-gun!"

"Say," I told him, "that horse *did* cheapen up, didn't he?"

This showed my friend that good doggers and hazers have to be worked on as much, or more, as any horses you'll use at a rodeo. You won't find just *any* horse that'll do for this event.

They've got to have almost as much speed as a racing Quarter Horse and as much endurance as an old Spanish Mustang.

Bulldogging horses are about the only ponies you'll find that rodeo cowboys will get out and race for the fun of it. And I've seen rodeos where one dogging horse carried every bulldogger in that performance. They may run 10 or 15 steers, one after the other. And one time I hazed 36 steers off the same horse, in two performances, the same day at a rodeo at Sidney, Iowa.

You can see you'd need a good stout horse for both jobs. But your dogging horse can be smaller than the hazing horse, not over 14.1 or 14.2 hands high. On a small horse, the bulldogger won't have so far to jump.

Then too, a little low, heavyset horse won't sway so much when you put all your weight on one side. I've seen doggers that weighed over 200 pounds grab that saddlehorn with their left hands and just hang down on the horse, then catch the steer as they went by it.

As your weight leaves the saddle, the horse should run out from under you, on past the steer, and set your feet down at an angle in front. Then you plow up some ground with your boots until you can throw the steer.

But if that horse slows or stops as you get off, your feet will be dragging the ground *behind* you—like the friend of mine who once tried to bulldog a steer off a motorcycle. He got all right after awhile.

The Hazing Horse

The other part of this team—the hazing horse—is just as important as the dogging horse. If you were to start down on that steer and the hazing horse wasn't there, the steer would just shy off to the right. That's when you might grab a mouthfull of dirt. So it's the job of the dogging horse to put you next to the steer and run on by. And it's the hazing horse's job to keep that steer going straight—to make sure it's there when you jump.

The worst thing I can think of is a small hazing horse you couldn't handle. He ought to be a big pony. Those steers get big too. And nowadays you find a lot of Florida steers in rodeos. They're just waspy as they can be. I've seen them jump when the dogging horse touched them, and kick the hazing horse—

so that's why you find lots of roping horses used for hazing. They can stop when they need to and get away fast, and they'll stand still until you're ready to go.

How A Dogging Team Scores

Here's how bulldogging and hazing horses earn their keep:

At most rodeos, you'll find only a few dogging teams. There may be over 100 bulldoggers and not over 20 horses for them to ride. Let's say I have a dogging team—well, I'll agree to let so many of the boys ride my dogging horse. I'll probably do the hazing myself, if I own the team. Each bulldogger who rides my horse agrees to pay me a fourth of what he wins in that event.

If none of them win anything, neither do I. But usually an owner of a team can figure on making some money if his horses are trained right. And the bulldoggers don't have to worry about the cost of hauling the horse from one show to another.

If you own this dogging team, the first thing you can figure on is that a lot of your bulldoggers won't be extra good riders. Some boys who can sure enough wrestle a steer don't spend much more time on a horse than it takes to catch a steer. That's why your dogging horse can't be temperamental. He's got to get used to every kind of rider that comes along.

So now let's see what happens—or what's *supposed* to happen—in running this event.

Your steer will come out of a chute, in most rodeos, that's not much different from the chute in calf roping. The bull-dogging horse and rider will be on the steer's left, the hazing horse and rider on its right.

There will be a string or elastic barrier across in front of the dogging horse—that's to make sure you give the steer whatever head start that rodeo says to give it. That'll be from six feet to 30 feet.

The hazing horse doesn't have a barrier in front of him. But he sure can't start after a steer before the dogging horse. If he does, it may cause the steer to duck in front of the dogger.

Both horses need to be calm and stand beside that chute and not jump when the gate rattles. The bulldogger is the one who asks for the steer to be turned out—he's the one who'll try to catch him.

When the steer leaves the chute, he belongs to the dogger, even if he gets out of the arena. When this happens—and once in awhile it does—they stop the watch until the steer can be caught and put back in the chute. Then the dogger can try it again. This time there's no barrier, and the time it takes him to throw the steer will be added to the time before, when the steer got out of the arena.

This could finally run into a pretty good day's work. The only reason you'd want to try the steer again is if you're still in the "average."

Now if you dive off and miss the steer and feel like another try, the hazer can come back and let you use his horse—or in some rodeos, he can bring your horse back to you. But you have to jump onto that steer from horseback. The clock stops when the steer hits the ground and all four feet are pointed the same way.

Do's And Don'ts of Bulldogging

In picking a horse I'd want for dogging or hazing, the first thing I'd think about would be speed. Both will have to be horses with lots of speed for at least 100 yards—the length of most rodeo arenas.

Except in Cheyenne. There, it's close to 200 yards. They give the steers a 30 foot start and you can think of every mean thing you've ever done before you can catch up with that steer. If you win bulldogging money at Cheyenne you won't have to *ask* anybody if you had a good horse. You'll *know* you did.

Most of your bulldoggers that go for the big money spend a lot of time picking the horses they want to buy. They'll watch horses at rodeos for maybe a couple of years before they decide what to buy. They'll see how different horses work with all kinds of riders.

And they'll try to get a dogging horse around seven years old. He'll be in his prime from then until he's about 14.

There's some things you want to make sure you work on in getting a bulldogging team ready to compete.

First, as I said before, the dogging horse has to speed up as you dive on the steer. Once you work a dogging team together much, the dogging horse will follow the hazing horse on to the end of the arena. These horses get to be pretty crazy about each other and they like to stay together.

Second, the team should be worked on all kinds of steers to make sure they'll go any way a steer may try to go. If the steer heads for one fence or the other, both horses have to cut fast, to head the steer on down the arena, and still give the dogger room to make his jump. And one of the worst falls you can take is when your dogging horse overshoots the steer—cuts in front of it as you're leaving the saddle.

When this happens, there's no time to do much but hope. I've been run over lots of times and so have most rodeo cowboys. It's surprising more don't get hurt. Some can even laugh about it later.

One time I saw a fellow named Bill Hancock take a dive for a steer and go over the steer's back. Jumped clean over it and hit right in front of the hazing horse. As Bill hit the ground and the horse ran over him, the hazer yelled: "Hey, look out!"

Bill raised up out of the dirt and called out after him: "What are you gonna do—come back *again?*"

It's probably true that lots of bulldoggers worry as much about their horses as they do themselves. They'll go to some trouble to make sure a dogging horse is shod right, for instance. You want to shoe him "short," to where he won't catch his feet. Fast-breaking horses can pull a shoe off as they get away from a chute—especially if they're running in mud, sand or grass.

And you'd want to ride a dogging horse with a bit that won't hurt his mouth. A snaffle bit with a shank on it is good. A rough bit can ruin a good dogging horse, if a lot of different doggers ride him. This is because some young riders will start to get down on a steer, decide to wait a minute and pull themselves back up with the reins. If a horse is bitted rough, a few hard runs like that can make him pretty upset and spooky.

I've seen lots of good doggers drop the reins of a well-trained dogging horse as they left the chute. The horse knew what to do and did it. The riders just went along until time to make their jump.

Finally . . .

Every day you won't feel the same about your horse. Maybe you won't have time to use him every day. You should try to, though. Especially when you get disgusted with something *else* you've been doing.

You'll get a lot of pleasure and relaxation when you get back to your horse. He'll make you forget your troubles for awhile. And if I were going to give you one last word of advice, I think it would be this:

Try to have as much patience
with your horse as you want
him to have with you.

ACKNOWLEDGMENTS

Lots of people, over a period of months, helped gather statistics and background material for this book. They helped in other ways too. Some gave advice, others gave their time and encouragement, still others offered sympathy. At times it was all needed.

So we want to thank especially:

The American Quarter Horse Association and Quarter Horse Journal staff, the Rodeo Cowboy's Association, Breeder's Gazette, Butler-Johnson Corporation, Mrs. Billy Alice Johnson, Lester Goodson, J. B. Ferguson, Pinehurst Stables, Doyle Gougler, Dick Darby, Pam Taylor, Rex Cauble, Milt Bennett and Louis Cauble.

Photo Credits:
Owen Johnson,
The Houston Post..........Page 13, 20 and End Sheets
American Quarter Horse Association...........Page 18
Wiley Smith...........................Page 82 and 83
Jim Keeland...............................Page 77
Orren Mixer.........................Page 7 and 8
Herman Baty, Mexia, Texas.................Page 84
Bob Gray—all other photographs
Cover: "Paul A." Photo by Harold Israel.

Art by Bob Schoenke